THE BROAD AUTISM PHENOTYPE

ADVANCES IN SPECIAL EDUCATION

Series Editor: Anthony F. Rotatori

Recent Volumes:

Volume 21: History of Special Education – Edited by Anthony F. Rotatori, Festus E. Obiakor, and Jeffrey P. Bakken

Volume 22: Behavioral Disorders: Identification, Assessment, and Instruction of Students with EBD – Edited by Jeffrey P. Bakken, Festus E. Obiakor, and Anthony F. Rotatori

Volume 23: Behavioral Disorders: Practice Concerns and Students with EBD – Edited by Jeffrey P. Bakken, Festus E. Obiakor, and Anthony F. Rotatori

Volume 24: Learning Disabilities: Identification, Assessment, and Instruction of Students with LD – Edited by Jeffrey P. Bakken, Festus E. Obiakor, and Anthony F. Rotatori

Volume 25: Learning Disabilities: Practice Concerns and Students with LD – Edited by Jeffrey P. Bakken, Festus E. Obiakor, and Anthony F. Rotatori

Volume 26: Gifted Education: Current Perspectives and Issues – Edited by Jeffrey P. Bakken, Festus E. Obiakor, and Anthony F. Rotatori

Volume 27: Special Education International Perspectives: Biopsychosocial, Cultural, and Disability Aspects – Edited by Anthony F. Rotatori, Jeffrey P. Bakken, Sandra Burkhardt, Festus E. Obiakor, and Umesh Sharma

Volume 28: Special Education International Perspectives: Practices Across the Globe – Edited by Anthony F. Rotatori, Jeffrey P. Bakken, Sandra Burkhardt, Festus E. Obiakor, and Umesh Sharma

ADVANCES IN SPECIAL EDUCATION   VOLUME 29

THE BROAD AUTISM PHENOTYPE

BY

JULIE A. DEISINGER

Department of Psychology, Saint Xavier University, Chicago, IL, USA

EDITED BY

ANTHONY F. ROTATORI

Department of Psychology, Saint Xavier University, Chicago, IL, USA

United Kingdom – North America – Japan
India – Malaysia – China

Emerald Group Publishing Limited
Howard House, Wagon Lane, Bingley BD16 1WA, UK

First edition 2015

Copyright © 2015 Emerald Group Publishing Limited

Reprints and permissions service
Contact: permissions@emeraldinsight.com

No part of this book may be reproduced, stored in a retrieval system, transmitted in any form or by any means electronic, mechanical, photocopying, recording or otherwise without either the prior written permission of the publisher or a licence permitting restricted copying issued in the UK by The Copyright Licensing Agency and in the USA by The Copyright Clearance Center. Any opinions expressed in the chapters are those of the authors. Whilst Emerald makes every effort to ensure the quality and accuracy of its content, Emerald makes no representation implied or otherwise, as to the chapters' suitability and application and disclaims any warranties, express or implied, to their use.

British Library Cataloguing in Publication Data
A catalogue record for this book is available from the British Library

ISBN: 978-1-78441-658-4
ISSN: 0270-4013 (Series)

ISOQAR certified Management System, awarded to Emerald for adherence to Environmental standard ISO 14001:2004.

Certificate Number 1985
ISO 14001

INVESTOR IN PEOPLE

This book is respectfully dedicated to the participants of the studies described in its contents, and to the researchers whose work has increased our understanding of them.

CONTENTS

FOREWORD ix

1. RECOGNITION OF THE BROAD AUTISM PHENOTYPE 1
   References 7

2. IDENTIFICATION AND ASSESSMENT OF THE BROAD AUTISM PHENOTYPE 9
   2.1. Utilization of the *Diagnostic and Statistical Manual of Mental Disorders* 9
   2.2. Utilization of Measurement Tools 11
   References 29

3. GENETIC ASPECTS OF THE BROAD AUTISM PHENOTYPE 37
   3.1. Family Studies 38
   3.2. Simplex versus Multiplex Family Studies 42
   3.3. Twin Studies 46
   3.4. Endophenotypes 48
   3.5. Molecular Genetic Studies 55
   References 58

4. OTHER BIOLOGICAL ASPECTS OF THE BROAD AUTISM PHENOTYPE 65
   4.1. Differences in Brain Structure 65
   4.2. Differences in Brain Function 67
   4.3. Differences in Head Circumference 72
   4.4. Possible Differences in Immune System Functioning 74
   4.5. Other Biological Differences in the BAP 77
   4.6. Summary 78
   References 79

5. **COGNITIVE FUNCTIONING IN THE BROAD AUTISM PHENOTYPE** — *83*
  5.1. Perception and Visual Attention — *83*
  5.2. Face Processing — *91*
  5.3. Phonological Processing — *98*
  5.4. Language Ability — *100*
  5.5. Intellectual Functioning — *104*
  5.6. Executive Functioning — *106*
  5.7. Central Coherence — *109*
  5.8. Theory of Mind (ToM) — *111*
  5.9. Social Cognition — *118*
  5.10. Summary — *121*
  References — *121*

FOREWORD

The Diagnostic and Statistical Manual of Mental Disorders (DSM; American Psychiatric Association, 2000) specifies that Autism Spectrum Disorder (ASD) is a complex neurodevelopmental disorder that comprises a group of conditions which include the following: Autistic disorder, Asperger disorder, childhood disintegrative disorder, Rett's disorder, and pervasive developmental disorder not otherwise specified. The Center for Disease Control (CDC, 2012) reports that ASD is increasing rapidly with more than one percent of the global population having this disorder. Over the past twenty years, many advances have been made in examining the causes for the disorder; developing accurate identification and diagnostic procedures; validating best practices to instruct children with this disorder; and implementing evidence based social-emotional and behavioral treatment methods (Deisinger, 2012). However, ASD remains a significant worldwide public health issue (Johnson, 2014; WHO, 2013).

Positively, considerable research findings have supported the understanding that ASD is a neurodevelopmental disorder which is characterized by deficits in language and social-emotional functioning and markedly restricted interest and activities (American Psychiatric Association, 2013). These investigations have led to findings that point to the role of genetic factors in the etiology of ASD (Deisinger, 2012). More pointedly, considerable investigations have occurred related to identifying behavioral markers of vulnerability to ASD for the following domains: language, personality, cognitive, and social-emotional. With the advent of new technologies and methods, there has been considerable investigative progress and relevant findings in the past decade regarding knowledge about the association between these behavioral markers and the genetic causes of ASD (Deisinger, 2012). Findings about this association have come from twin and family studies (Hoekstra, Van Beijsterveldt, & Boomsma, 2007), studies about genetic syndromes linked with ASD (Aitken, 2010), and molecular studies of ASD genetics (Aitken, 2010). More importantly, these literature findings point to a constellation of language, cognition, social, and personality characteristics that parallel the defining features of ASD which are currently being referenced in the literature as Broad Autism Phenotype (Sasson, Lam, Parlier, Daniels, & Piven, 2013).

This volume, The Broad Autism Phenotype, provides readers with in-depth coverage about the broad autism phenotype (BAP). This volume describes in detail the BAP which encompasses biological, cognitive, emotional, behavioral, and interpersonal characteristics resembling those found on the autism spectrum, although more subtle than what is evident among individuals who meet formal criteria for an autism spectrum diagnosis. Initially identified in 1944, the BAP has been receiving increased attention due to the recognition of autism as a spectrum of disorders that vary in symptoms and severity. Researchers believe that studying the BAP may yield helpful information concerning the etiology and early identification of autism.

Chapter 1 of this volume opens with a definition of the BAP, a description of its historical origins, insight into a better understanding of BAP related to its defining elements and boundaries as well as a discussion about a lack of consensus among researchers and professionals regarding what constellation of traits compose the BAP and the variety of measures that are used to investigate it.

Chapter 2 provides a comprehensive examination concerned with the identification and assessment of the BAP. It includes descriptions and critiques of currently used devices and procedures such as interviews, observational approaches, rating scales, checklists, and questionnaires. The chapter author points out while a variety of procedures and devices are available, the detection of the BAP can be challenging due to the lack of uniformity in the way that clinicians and scientists define it, as well as the differing ways that it manifests in males and females. Also, different assessment devices emphasis different aspects of the BAP. As such the chapter's author stresses that the optimal assessment of the BAP should include self reports, information from multiple sources, and direct clinical observations.

Chapter 3 provides a thorough review of genetic aspects of the BAP. The author delineates findings from family and simplex versus multiplex family studies and twin studies. Then, the author discusses endophenotypes which are inherited quantitative phenotypic components of a syndrome (Constantino, 2011). Endophenotypes may be physiological, behavioral, or neuropsychological and are evident in both affected and unaffected individuals (Constantino, 2011). Lastly, the chapter provides a review of molecular genetic studies concerned with the examination of phenotypes due to either gene-gene or gene-environment interactions. The author emphasizes that the gene-environment aspects associated with BAP is very valuable due to the identification of environmental factors that might be present during prenatal and neonatal development as the identification of these factors would increase the possibility of directing efforts toward the prevention of ASD (Jensen, 2013).

In chapter 4, the author presents information about other biological characteristics of the BAP. The chapter is divided into three sections, namely, differences in brain anatomical structure and function as it relates to the BAP, the relationship between head circumference and the BAP, and the association between the immune system functioning and the BAP. The author points out that recent studies concerned with the above reveal that the BAP involves a variety of biological features that differ from what is found among the general population. These features include: structural differences in both cortical and subcortical regions of the brain which in turn may be linked to atypical activity in the frontal cortex and in areas that are responsible for the processing of social stimuli; and increases in head circumference, levels of whole blood serotonin and testosterone, and rates of obstetric complications. Lastly, the author indicates that while some studies have suggested that autoimmune disorders and epilepsy may be associated with the BAP current research is inconclusive regarding the association between these conditions and the BAP.

Chapter 5 provides an in-depth analysis of the cognitive functioning in the BAP. It focuses on various types of cognitive functioning that have been explored among people with ASD which include the following: perceptual and visual attention, face processing, phonological processing, language ability, intellectual functioning, and executive functioning. In addition, the chapter explores theories more specifically to ASD, namely, central coherence, theories of mind, and social cognition. The author's chapter summary of the available research indicates that individuals with the BAP may engage in atypical processing of sensory information and exhibit unusual patterns of visual orienting and that impaired phonological processing may be an element of the BAP. Further, the intelligence among individuals with BAP is variable and it is unclear whether deficits in executive functioning, central coherence, or theories of mind should be considered characteristics of the BAP. Lastly, studies conducted within the last decade appear to indicate that BAP includes reduced ability for social cognition.

This volume provides autism professionals and researchers with a comprehensive overview of research about the broad autism phenotype from its earliest recognition until the present time. In addition to an academic readership, the book illuminates information about the broad autism phenotype that may be of interest to family members of individuals on the autism spectrum.

Anthony F. Rotatori
Series Editor

REFERENCES

American Psychiatric Association. (2000). *Diagnostic and statistical manual of mental disorders* (4th ed.). Washington, DC: Author.
American Psychiatric Association. (2013). *Diagnostic and statistical manual of mental disorders* (5th ed.). Arlington, VA: Author.
Aitken, K. J. (2010). *An A-Z of genetics factors in autism: A handbook for parents and carers*. Philadelphia, PA: Jessica Kingsley.
Center for Disease Control and Prevention. (2012). *Prevalence of autism spectrum disorders and developmental disabilities monitoring network, 14 sites, United States, 2008* (Vol. 61, No. 3), Surveillance Summaries.
Constantino, J. N. (2011). The quantitative nature of autistic social impairment. *Pediatric Research, 69*, 55–62.
Deisinger, J. (2012). Genetic factors associated with autism spectrum disorders. In J. Deisinger, S. Burkhardt, T. Wahlberg, A. F. Rotatori, & F. E. Obiakor (Eds.), *Autism spectrum disorders: Inclusive community for the twenty-first century* (pp. 75–111). Charlotte, NC: Information Age Publishing, Inc.
Hoekstra, R. A., Van Beijsterveldt, T. O., & Boomsma, D. I. (2007). Genetics and environmental covariation between autistic traits and behavioral problems. *Twin Research and Human Genetics, 10*(6), 853–860.
Jensen, R. A. (2013). The background genetic effect of the genes underlying the broad autism phenotype as a unifying feature in gene x and gene x environment causal mechanisms in autism. *O.A. Autism, 1*(2), 11–18.
Johnson, E. (2014). Autism spectrum disorders: The worldwide charm and challenge of autism spectrum disorder. In A. F. Rotatori, J. P. Bakken, S. Burkhardt, F. E. Obiakor, & U. Sharma (Eds.), *Special education international perspectives: Biopsychosocial, cultural and disability aspects* (Vol. 27, pp. 117–151). Advances in Special Education. Bingley, UK: Emerald Group Publishing Limited.
Sasson, N. J., Lam, K. S. L., Parlier, M., Daniels, J. L., & Piven, J. (2013). Autism and the broad autism phenotype: Familial and intergenerational transmission. *Journal of Neurodevelopmental Disorders, 5*(1), 11.
World Health Organization (WHO). (2013). *International Classification of Diseases (ICD) information sheet*. Retrieved from http:www.who.int/classification/icd/factsheet/en/index.html

CHAPTER 1

RECOGNITION OF THE BROAD AUTISM PHENOTYPE

The term "broad autism phenotype," or BAP, refers to a condition involving milder forms of traits that are commonly associated with autism spectrum disorders (ASD), such as communication deficits, behavioral routines, and distaste for change (Roth, 2010). Additionally, the BAP includes social aloofness, predilections for anxiety and depression, and cognitive weaknesses in the forms of problems with reading comprehension, automatized naming, and executive functioning (Piven, 1997). Impulsivity, irritability, diminished positive affect, a lack of tact, and heightened sensitivity to criticism also may be components of the BAP (Cassel et al., 2007; Piven, 1997; Scheeren & Stauder, 2008).

The history of the BAP dates back to the pioneering work of Leo Kanner, who first identified autism as a separate developmental disorder (Losh, Adolphs, & Piven, 2011; Wolff, 2004). Kanner's 1943 publication called "Autistic Disturbances of Affective Content" used Eugen Bleuler's term "autism" to signify a state of self-absorption, yet it distinguished autism from childhood schizophrenia. As described in Kanner's groundbreaking paper, childhood schizophrenia constituted a state of regression that followed initially normal development; in contrast, autism represented a deviation from typical development that was apparent even in infancy (Folstein & Rutter, 1977; Goldstein & Ozonoff, 2009).

During his initial study of 11 children with autism, Kanner noticed that their parents were intelligent and successful in school and work. He also reported that although these parents displayed interests in science, art, and literature, they seemed less interested in other people (Neumarker, 2003; Wolff, 2004). Kanner's observations implied a set of features sometimes found among close relatives of people on the autism spectrum (Roth, 2010), which later would be dubbed the BAP.

A contemporary of Kanner named Hans Asperger also mentioned the existence of unusual characteristics in some parents of children with high-functioning autism. However, the two men differed in their assumptions about the meaning of these characteristics. Reflecting the dominant influence of psychoanalysis during the early twentieth century, Kanner initially believed that autism resulted from being raised in an environment that lacked parental warmth. In contrast, Asperger hypothesized that autistic traits were likely to be biologically transmitted from parent to child (Roth, 2010).

More than 30 years after Kanner's seminal article, Folstein and Rutter (1977) conducted a twin study which firmly implicated genetic factors as important in the etiology of autism. These investigators pointed out that autism was a rare condition with a population frequency of roughly two to four children per 10,000. However, among families in which one child had autism, 2% of siblings also had autism. Folstein and Rutter wrote that this rate of occurrence was 50 times the rate of autism in the general population, and they interpreted this finding as an indication that autism could involve genetic causal factors. These authors also reviewed the existing literature and found twin studies of autism, but noticed that the earlier studies often failed to include important details. For example, previous studies often did not state whether twin pairs were mono- or dizygotic, and many of them neglected to provide obstetric information that might link the etiology of autism to an environmental factor.

Folstein and Rutter (1977) performed a systematic investigation of 21 same-sex twin pairs in which at least one twin had autism. Among these, 11 were identical twin pairs and 10 were fraternal twin pairs. With regard to the identical twins, four pairs were found in which both twins had autism; however, none of the fraternal twin pairs contained two twins with autism. When applying a more relaxed definition of autism, these authors found that 82% of the identical twin pairs (9 of 11) were concordant for autism, whereas the same was true for only 10% of the fraternal twin pairs (1 of 10). Because identical twins are monozygotic they have the same genes, but fraternal or dizygotic twins are no more genetically similar than any other pair of siblings, that is, having only 50% of their genes in common (Roth, 2010). Thus, Folstein and Rutter concluded that the significantly higher rate of similarity among identical twins in comparison to fraternal twins "… clearly points strongly to the importance of genetic factors in the etiology of autism" (p. 307). However, they also reported that they could not determine the specific manner in which autism was transmitted, speculating that it might involve high mutation rates, polygenic inheritance, or other factors (Folstein & Rutter, 1977).

Folstein and Rutter's (1977) study was the first investigation to hint that the autism phenotype extended beyond the boundaries of classic autism (Losh et al., 2011; Piven, 2001). During the early 1990s, Joseph Piven and his associates (1991, 1994) began to further explore this notion by examining autism characteristics in family members of individuals with autism. They focused on parents of people with autism and compared them to parents of individuals with Down syndrome. When studying rates of psychiatric disorders in these two groups, Piven et al. (1991) discovered that parents of autism probands had a significantly higher prevalence of anxiety disorders than the comparison group and a significantly higher lifetime prevalence of major depressive disorder than the general population. Piven et al. (1994) assessed the personality features of these two samples and found that parents of persons with autism were much more likely to exhibit the traits of being aloof, unresponsive, and lacking in tactfulness. The findings from these studies lent further support to the idea that autism features could be identified in biological relatives of people with ASD.

In 1994 Patrick Bolton and his colleagues introduced the term "broader phenotype" (p. 879) into the scientific literature about autism. Bolton et al. (1994) were interested in learning more about the characteristics of what they called a "lesser variant of autism" (p. 877). To do so, they studied the families of 99 people with autism and compared them to the families of 36 people with Down syndrome. These researchers found that among cognitively unimpaired siblings of people with autism, from 12.4% to 20.4% of them exhibited milder forms of autistic traits such as repetitive behaviors and deficits in social functioning and language ability. Because autism-like characteristics frequently occurred among family members of autism index cases yet were found much less often among family members of Down syndrome probands, Bolton and associates (1994) surmised that genetic factors were responsible for the BAP.

Bailey et al. (1995) extended previous findings by conducting another twin study that included as many of the twin pairs as possible from the Folstein and Rutter (1977) study. They supplemented the previous sample with newly recruited twin pairs in which at least one twin had autism. The purpose of the 1995 investigation was to examine whether obstetric complications associated with autism were either an outcome of abnormal prenatal development or a possible causal factor for autism. Bailey and colleagues re-examined 10 monozygotic and 9 dizygotic twin pairs from the

1977 twin study, while adding 17 monozygotic and 11 dizygotic twin pairs to their participant sample. Upon combining these two samples, they found that 60% of identical (i.e., monozygotic) twins were concordant for autism whereas no fraternal (i.e., dizygotic) twins were concordant. Using a broader definition of autism, Bailey et al. found that 92% of identical twin pairs but only 10% of fraternal twin pairs were concordant for social and cognitive deficits. On the basis of their findings, Bailey and associates decided that obstetric problems linked with autism were most likely the result of atypical prenatal development. These researchers also stated that "... genetic influences may give rise to a phenotype considerably broader than autism as traditionally diagnosed" (p. 72).

In yet another twin study, Le Couteur et al. (1996) sought to clarify the parameters of the BAP. She and her colleagues formulated a definition of the BAP that encompassed both cognitive and social deficits. The cognitive deficits that they associated with the BAP included two or more of the following concerns: delayed language acquisition or problems with speech articulation, reading, or spelling. This research team defined social deficits of the BAP as involving two or more symptoms from among the following list: impaired social play and lack of affection toward caregivers during childhood, peculiar or socially unacceptable behavior in adulthood, and social isolation or impaired conversational ability throughout life. Le Couteur and colleagues indicated that for the purposes of their study, the BAP was comprised of either impaired communication or impaired social function, or both. Although they assessed their sample for the presence of repetitive behaviors, they chose not to include stereotyped behaviors in their definition of the BAP.

Participants in the Le Couteur et al. (1996) study again were twin pairs from Folstein and Rutter's (1977) research, as well as twin pairs from Bailey et al.'s (1995) study. Twenty-eight pairs were monozygotic and 20 were same-sex dizygotic twin pairs. Among these pairings, Le Couteur and associates looked for twin pairs that were discordant for full-blown autism. They detected the BAP in seven of nine identical twin pairs in which one twin had classic autism and the other did not. In comparison, the BAP was identified in only 2 of 20 fraternal twin pairs that were discordant for traditionally defined autism. Statistical analysis revealed that this difference between identical versus fraternal twin pairs was highly significant. The research team concluded that "... phenotypic expression extends more broadly than autism as currently defined ..." (p. 793).

Piven, Palmer, Jacobi, Childress, and Arndt (1997) built on prior research of the BAP by studying families in which more than one person was diagnosed with autism. Such multiple-incidence autism families had not been previously investigated for the presence of the BAP. Piven, Palmer, Jacobi, et al. (1997) recruited parents from 25 families in which at least two children had autism; the comparison group consisted of parents from 30 families who had a child with Down syndrome. The researchers evaluated these parents for the presence of impaired communication, social deficits, rigidity, and circumscribed interests. Results yielded significant differences between the two groups, with higher rates of BAP characteristics found among the parents of multiple-incidence autism families. Also that year, Piven, Palmer, Landa, et al. (1997) specifically explored language and personality features in parents who had more than one child with autism. Once again, parents who had a child with Down syndrome served as a comparison group. When compared to parents of Down syndrome children, parents who had two children with autism demonstrated more problems with pragmatic language, had fewer friendships, and were more likely to have personality traits such as aloofness, anxiousness, rigidity, and heightened sensitivity to criticism. Piven, Palmer, Jacobi, et al. (1997) and Piven, Palmer, Landa, et al. (1997) urged future investigators to consider the BAP when conducting genetic studies of autism.

Cognitive functioning in the immediate relatives of people with autism was the focus of a study by Fombonne, Bolton, Prior, Jordan, and Rutter (1997). Fombonne and associates recruited parents and siblings from families in which at least one person had autism, and used family members of individuals with Down syndrome for purposes of comparison. They interviewed participants to inquire about the presence of impaired communication or social functioning as well as stereotyped behavior. Participants also completed tests of intellectual functioning, reading ability, and spelling ability. Fombonne et al. found no increase in the incidence of extremely low intellectual functioning among non-autistic first-degree relatives of autism probands. Instead, they discovered that autism relatives tended to have higher verbal intelligence, although BAP siblings of children with autism had lower intelligence quotients and performed less well on tests of reading and spelling than non-BAP siblings of individuals with ASD. This study did not uncover any cognitive differences among parents with the BAP. Based on their inability to identify a specific cognitive profile among first-degree relatives of autism probands, Fombonne and colleagues cautioned that the use of standardized measures of cognitive functioning might not be helpful in creating an operational definition of the BAP.

Seeking to summarize what was known about the expression of autism among relatives, Bailey, Palferman, Heavey, and Le Couteur (1998) published a review article that detailed the kinds of abnormalities associated with "milder phenotypic expression" (p. 379). These authors listed a preference for solitude, having few friends, poor conversational skills, and deficits in affection, empathy, and tact as social impairments that were typically observed in parents and siblings of individuals with autism. Communication impairments that they reported among first-degree relatives of autism probands included language delays, problems with speech articulation, and difficulties with reading and spelling. Concerning repetitive behaviors, Bailey et al. (1998) wrote that these could be found only in a small number of autism relatives, although a rigid personality reportedly was common in parents of children with autism. Psychiatric disorders that were often noticed in first-degree relatives of people with autism consisted of various anxiety disorders such as panic disorder, generalized anxiety disorder, obsessive-compulsive disorder, social phobia, and other phobic disorders. Mood disorders in the forms of both major depressive disorder and bipolar disorder also were seen in this group.

Bailey and associates (1998) highlighted the wide range of variability in both symptoms and symptom severity among relatives of people with autism, but wrote that the exact components of the BAP and their boundaries had not yet been precisely determined. They also could not determine whether milder expressions of the autism phenotype usually appear early in the course of development, and suggested that future research should include longitudinal studies to examine developmental change over time.

For the past 20 years, the BAP has received increasing attention from scientific investigators who believe that a better understanding of this entity may yield greater knowledge about the characteristics of autism (Losh et al., 2011). To that end, an important issue is the need for researchers to agree upon the BAP's defining elements and boundaries. Fombonne et al. (1997) attempted to distinguish between a mild and severe variant of the BAP. They defined the mild variant as involving atypicality in only one domain of autism symptoms, and viewed the severe variant as a combination of problems in two of the three traditional symptom clusters for ASD (i.e., social functioning, communication ability, and repetitive behaviors). Similarly, Wheelwright, Auyeung, Allison, and Baron-Cohen (2010) used the concepts of narrow autism phenotype (NAP) and medium autism phenotype (MAP) to differentiate these from the BAP. According to Wheelwright et al. (2010), the NAP involves many traits commonly found in autism, as measured by a score of three or more standard deviations above the mean on a self-report instrument called the Autism-Spectrum Quotient (AQ; Baron-Cohen, Wheelwright, Skinner, Martin, & Clubley,

2001). Most people with the NAP are likely to have received an autism diagnosis. Individuals with the MAP have fewer autism traits than the NAP but more than the BAP. MAP individuals obtain AQ scores that are two to three standard deviations above the mean on the AQ, while those with the BAP score only one to two standard deviations above the mean on this questionnaire (Wheelwright et al., 2010). Wheelwright and colleagues (2010) suspected that people who meet criteria for either the MAP or BAP may have no need for therapeutic intervention, yet studies of their genetic make-up still might shed valuable light on the genetics of the ASD.

Although an operational definition of the BAP might be possible through the use of a particular psychometric instrument like the AQ, other researchers indicate that currently there is no uniform definition of the BAP (Losh et al., 2011; Scheeren & Stauder, 2008). Scheeren and Stauder (2008) observed that most BAP research has examined some combination of social impairment, communication problems, and restricted or repetitive behaviors. Losh et al. (2011) further noted that the lack of consensus about BAP traits and the variety of measures that are used to investigate it complicate scientists' ability to incorporate the BAP in genetic studies.

REFERENCES

Bailey, A., Le Couteur, A., Gottesman, I., Bolton, P., Simonoff, E., Yuzda, E., & Rutter, M. (1995). Autism as a strongly genetic disorder: Evidence from a British twin study. *Psychological Medicine*, *25*(1), 63–77. doi:10.1017/S0033291700028099

Bailey, A., Palferman, S., Heavey, L., & Le Couteur, A. (1998). Autism: The phenotype in relatives. *Journal of Autism and Developmental Disorders*, *28*(5), 369–392. doi:10.1023/A:1026048320785

Baron-Cohen, S., Wheelwright, S., Skinner, R., Martin, J., & Clubley, E. (2001). The Autism-Spectrum Quotient (AQ): Evidence from Asperger syndrome/high-functioning autism, males and females, scientists and mathematicians. *Journal of Autism and Developmental Disorders*, *31*(1), 5–17. doi:10.1023/A:1005653411471

Bolton, P., Macdonald, H., Pickles, A., Rios, P., Goode, S., Crowson, M., ... Rutter, M. (1994). A case-control family history study of autism. *Journal of Child Psychology and Psychiatry*, *35*(5), 877–900. doi:10.1111/j.1469-7610.1994.tb02300.x

Cassel, T. D., Messinger, D. S., Ibanez, L. V., Haltigan, J. D., Acosta, S. I., & Buchman, A. C. (2007). Early social and emotional communication in the infant siblings of children with autism spectrum disorders: An examination of the broad phenotype. *Journal of Autism and Developmental Disorders*, *37*(1), 122–132. doi:10.1007/s10803-006-0337-1

Folstein, S., & Rutter, M. (1977). Infantile autism: A genetic study of 21 twin pairs. *Journal of Child Psychology and Psychiatry*, *18*(4), 297–321. doi:10.1111/j.1469-7610.1977.tb00443.x

Fombonne, E., Bolton, P., Prior, J., Jordan, H., & Rutter, M. (1997). A family study of autism: Cognitive patterns and levels in parents and siblings. *Journal of Child Psychology and Psychiatry, 38*(6), 667–683. doi:10.1111/j.1469-7610.1997.tb01694.x

Goldstein, S., & Ozonoff, S. (2009). Historical perspective and overview. In S. Goldstein, J. A. Naglieri, & S. Ozonoff (Eds.), *Assessment of autism spectrum disorders* (pp. 1–17). New York, NY: Guilford Press.

Le Couteur, A., Bailey, A., Goode, S., Pickles, A., Robertson, S., Gottesman, I., & Rutter, M. (1996). A broader phenotype of autism: The clinical spectrum in twins. *Journal of Child Psychology and Psychiatry, 37*(7), 785–801. doi:10.1111/j.1469-7610.1996.tb01475.x

Losh, M., Adolphs, R., & Piven, J. (2011). The broad autism phenotype. In D. G. Amaral, G. Dawson, & D. H. Geschwind (Eds.), *Autism spectrum disorders* (pp. 457–476). New York, NY: Oxford University Press, Inc.

Neumarker, K. J. (2003). Leo Kanner: His years in Berlin, 1906–24. The roots of autistic disorder. *History of Psychiatry, 14*(2), 205–218. doi:10.1177/0957154X030142005

Piven, J. (1997). The biological basis of autism. *Current Opinion in Neurobiology, 7*(5), 708–712. doi:10.1016/S0959-4388(97)80093-1

Piven, J. (2001). The broad autism phenotype: A complementary strategy for molecular genetic studies of autism. *American Journal of Medical Genetics (Neuropsychiatric Genetics), 105*, 34–35. doi:10.1002/1096-8628(20010108)

Piven, J., Chase, G. A., Landa, R., Wrozek, M., Gayle, J., Cloud, D., & Folstein, S. (1991). Psychiatric disorders in the parents of autistic individuals. *Journal of the American Academy of Child and Adolescent Psychiatry, 30*(3), 471–478. doi:10.1097/00004583-199105000-00019

Piven, J., Palmer, P., Jacobi, D., Childress, D., & Arndt, S. (1997). Broader autism phenotype: Evidence from a family history study of multiple-incidence autism families. *American Journal of Psychiatry, 154*(2), 185–190.

Piven, J., Palmer, P., Landa, R., Santangelo, S., Jacobi, D., & Childress, D. (1997). Personality and language characteristics in parents from multiple-incidence autism families. *American Journal of Medical Genetics, 74*(4), 398–411. doi:10.1002/(SICI)1096-8628(19970725)74:4<398::AID-AJMG11>3.0.CO;2-D

Piven, J., Wrozek, M., Landa, R., Lainhart, J., Bolton, P., Chase, G. A., & Folstein, S. (1994). Personality characteristics of the parents of autistic individuals. *Psychological Medicine, 24*(3), 783–795. doi:10.1017/S0033291700027938

Roth, I. (2010). *The autism spectrum in the 21st century: Exploring psychology, biology and practice*. Philadelphia, PA: Jessica Kingsley Publishers.

Scheeren, A. M., & Stauder, J. E. A. (2008). Broader autism phenotype in parents of autistic children: Reality or myth? *Journal of Autism and Developmental Disorders, 38*(2), 276–287. doi:10.1007/s10803-007-0389-x

Wheelwright, S., Auyeung, B., Allison, C., & Baron-Cohen, S. (2010). Defining the broader, medium and narrow autism phenotype among parents using the Autism Spectrum Quotient (AQ). *Molecular Autism, 1,* 10. (Open access article). doi:10.1186/2040-2393-1-10

Wolff, S. (2004). The history of autism. *European Child and Adolescent Psychiatry, 13*(4), 201–208. doi:10.1007/s00787-004-0363-5

CHAPTER 2

IDENTIFICATION AND ASSESSMENT OF THE BROAD AUTISM PHENOTYPE

2.1. UTILIZATION OF THE *DIAGNOSTIC AND STATISTICAL MANUAL OF MENTAL DISORDERS*

As outlined in the fifth edition of the *Diagnostic and Statistical Manual of Mental Disorders* (*DSM-5*; American Psychiatric Association (APA), 2013), the label of autism spectrum disorder (ASD) applies to persons who exhibit impaired social communication as well as restricted or repetitive behaviors and interests. Additionally, these symptoms must cause impairment in relationships, work, or other important areas of life (e.g., academic performance). Further clinical information can be obtained from specifiers indicating whether a person with ASD suffers from comorbid catatonia or has impairments in intelligence or language. Specifiers also denote whether someone's ASD results from an identifiable genetic, medical, or environmental factor (APA, 2013).

The *DSM-5* emphasizes the variability of ASD, reporting that this category consists of "... disorders previously referred to as early infantile autism, childhood autism, Kanner's autism, high-functioning autism, atypical autism, pervasive developmental disorder not otherwise specified, childhood disintegrative disorder, and Asperger's disorder" (APA, 2013, p. 53). The removal from *DSM-5* of separate diagnoses for Asperger's disorder and pervasive developmental disorder not otherwise specified has received considerable attention and has elicited some concern among people with ASDs, their families, and the clinicians who treat them (e.g., see Buxbaum & Baron-Cohen, 2013; Lai, Lombardo, Chakrabarti, & Baron-Cohen, 2013; Ne'eman & Kapp, 2012). However, empirical evidence supports this major change in the psychiatric manual, at least in the United States and the United Kingdom (Duku et al., 2013; Mandy, Charman, Puura, & Skuse, 2014). For example, a study by Lord et al. (2012) examined diagnoses given by expert clinicians at 12 university-affiliated autism centers and discovered a lack of reliability in the way that subcategories of ASD were assigned. Such findings underscore the fact that autism truly is a spectrum of disorders with many different manifestations (Georgiades et al., 2013; Lai et al., 2013).

Also, a factor-analytic study by Duku and associates (2013) examined multiple models of the ASD phenotype using scores from the Autism Diagnostic Interview-Revised (ADI-R; Lord, Rutter, & Le Couteur, 1994) that were obtained from a large sample of over 3,600 participants. Although a six-factor model seemed to best describe the ASD phenotype, Duku et al. found that "... the two-factor model provided a good fit to the data for the ASD group as a whole" (p. 8). In other words, their results support the *DSM-5* model of ASD which depends on the presence of two symptom groups: social communication deficits, and restricted interests or repetitive behaviors (APA, 2013).

No mention of the broad autism phenotype (BAP) appears in the *DSM-5* (Rutter, 2013). Its absence in the current diagnostic manual seems appropriate. By definition the BAP involves only some but not all features of ASD and these do not lead to functional impairment, whereas symptoms that cause impairment in major life domains would be required for a clinical diagnosis (Gerdts & Bernier, 2011; Losh, Adolphs, & Piven, 2011). Nevertheless, at this time the boundary between ASD and the BAP is indistinct. As noted by Mandy and colleagues (2014), "there are no diagnostic biomarkers for autism spectrum disorder" (p. 45); consequently, ASD can be identified only on the basis of visible behaviors. Similarly, Mandy et al. (2014) pointed out that "there is no standardised, universal definition of the BAP, with no agreed cut-point to distinguish it from typical development" (p. 48). Lai et al. (2013) made a comparable observation, stating that "... the spectrum extends into the general population" (p. 5), which includes individuals with the BAP.

Mandy and associates (2014) wished to examine how well the *DSM-5* definition of ASD might apply to a subclinical population. In addition, they sought to determine whether the two-factor *DSM-5* model would generalize across cultures. These researchers located youngsters with the BAP in the United Kingdom and in Finland and gathered information about them using an instrument called the Developmental, Dimensional and Diagnostic Interview (3Di; Skuse et al., 2004). Upon performing confirmatory factor analyses, Mandy et al. found that the *DSM-5* model did fit the UK sample of individuals with the BAP; however, neither the *DSM-5* model nor other factor models generated by their analyses were a good fit for the Finnish BAP sample. Given this unexpected result, the investigators speculated that cultural influences might exert a more pronounced effect on milder autistic traits and recommended that future studies should explore this hypothesis further.

2.2. UTILIZATION OF MEASUREMENT TOOLS

Employing the *DSM-5* model of ASD is one possible way to identify people with the BAP, but measurement tools also have been created for this purpose. Interviews, observational approaches, rating scales, and questionnaires can be helpful for clinicians or scientists who wish to determine whether a given person meets criteria for the BAP. Such measures also might be used to detect specific traits or behaviors in order to identify strengths and weaknesses that may accompany the BAP.

2.2.1. Interviews

An interview was the earliest method used to detect the BAP among relatives of people with ASD. Rutter and Folstein (1995) created a semi-structured interview called the Family History Interview (FHI) for Developmental Disorders of Cognition and Social Functioning to gather information about parents and siblings of individuals with ASD. Bolton et al. (1994) used this interview, which they referred to as the Family History Schedule (FHS), in their examination of the BAP. This same designation (i.e., FHS) was used again by Fombonne, Bolton, Prior, Jordan, and Rutter (1997). Items from the FHI also were utilized in the following studies: Le Couteur et al. (1996), Piven, Palmer, Jacobi, Childress, and Arndt (1997a), Folstein et al. (1999), Mazefsky, Williams, and Minshew (2008), Pickles, St. Clair, and Conti-Ramsden (2013b). The first two of these investigations, as well as Fombonne et al. (1997), were described in Chapter 1. The latter studies are discussed in greater detail elsewhere in this book.

According to the brief descriptions that appear in the articles listed above, the FHI examines for the presence of communication difficulties, problems in social functioning, and restricted interests or stereotyped behaviors. In the realm of communication deficits, the FHI probes for information about speech delays, problems with speech articulation, and trouble with reading and spelling. Concerning social impairments, the FHI inquires about social isolation, abnormal play, deficient conversational ability, lack of emotional responsiveness toward caregivers, and socially inappropriate behavior (Le Couteur et al., 1996). Items pertaining to rigidity, perfectionism, restricted interests, obsessions, and compulsions assess for the presence of these symptoms in relatives of ASD probands (Bolton et al., 1994). The FHI also asks whether BAP symptoms are noticeable in both childhood and adulthood, due to its authors' recognition that some forms of social difficulty might become evident only in adolescence or later (Bolton et al., 1994).

Mazefsky et al. (2008) described the coding system used for the FHI. An item receives a score of 2 when its exact criteria as defined in the coding manual have been met. A score of 1 is given to signify that criteria probably have been met for an item. A score of 0 is assigned in three situations: (1) in cases of normal functioning; (2) in cases where the abnormal characteristics are mild; and (3) in situations where abnormalities exist but are not of the kind indicated in the manual.

Bolton and associates (1994) performed a confirmatory factor analysis to examine the validity of the FHI. They found that its three factors of communication problems, impaired social functioning, and stereotyped behavior were an excellent fit for capturing the dimensions of the BAP. On the basis of that analysis, they decided that the validity of the FHI was adequate. Pickles et al. (2013b) also described the FHI as "a reliable and valid schedule" (p. 159).

Another semi-structured interview that has been used to study the BAP is the Friendship Interview (FI). This measure was devised by an American research team led by Susan Folstein, in conjunction with British scientists under the supervision of Michael Rutter (Piven et al., 1997b; Santangelo & Folstein, 1995). The FI provides a way to assess someone's level of interest in establishing and maintaining friendships by inquiring about the number and quality of such relationships (Folstein et al., 1999; Piven et al., 1997b). It requests that interviewees name their three closest friends outside of their immediate family and answer several questions about the nature of these friendships (Piven et al., 1997b). In particular, one FI item rates the amount of reciprocal support in each of those friendships and another item rates the amount of information-sharing that takes place within them. Ratings for the amount of mutual support may range from 0 to 3, and ratings for the extent to which an interviewee confides in a friend range from 0 to 2. Scores from the three relationships on these two items are added together to yield a "friendship score" (Piven et al., 1997b, p. 403). Total scores on this portion of the FI may range from 0 to 15, with a score of 0 denoting high-quality friendships and a score of 15 signifying the absence of friendships (Losh, Childress, Lam, & Piven, 2008; Piven et al., 1997b).

Examining personality features of the BAP can be accomplished by administering a semi-structured interview called the Modified Personality Assessment Schedule-Revised (M-PAS-R; Piven et al., 1997b). Piven et al. (2013) referred to this instrument as one of the "preferred methods" for identifying the BAP among people who are 16 years of age and older (p. 3). The M-PAS-R derives from the Personality Assessment Schedule (PAS; Tyrer & Alexander, 1979; Tyrer, Alexander, Cicchetti, Cohen, & Remington, 1979), which was developed to identify personality disorders. When studying parents of children with ASD, Piven et al. (1994) altered the original PAS to make a modified version (M-PAS) that focused on 18 personality traits likely to be associated with the BAP. Piven et al. (1997b) further changed the M-PAS to the M-PAS-R by deleting 10 items that did not seem related to aspects of the BAP, and by expanding the definition of rigidity to better reflect the concept of resistance to new experiences. They also added optional questions to assist interviewers in determining whether a given trait was present, and made slight changes in the wording of some items to enhance clarity.

The M-PAS-R exists in a subject version that can be given directly to a person being assessed for the BAP, as well as an informant version that can be administered to someone well acquainted with the subject (e.g., a spouse). It asks about eight BAP features: goal-directed behavior, resistance to change, aloofness, restricted emotional expression, anxiety, heightened sensitivity to criticism, limited responses to emotional cues from others, and lack of tact (Piven et al., 1997b). Initially, Piven and colleagues (1997b) rated the intensity of each of these eight characteristics on a scale from 0 to 7; however, in order to improve interrater reliability, they abandoned this method. Instead, each characteristic is rated as either present or absent (Piven et al., 1997b). This instrument continues to be used in studies of the BAP (e.g., Lainhart et al., 2002; Losh, Esserman, & Piven, 2010; Losh et al., 2008, 2009; Piven et al., 2013; Smith et al., 2009).

A computerized interview measure that can be employed to assess features of the BAP is called the Developmental, Dimensional, and Diagnostic Interview, or 3Di (Skuse et al., 2004). Roth (2010) described its format as similar to that of a better known instrument, the Autism Diagnostic Interview (ADI; Le Couteur et al., 1989). Skuse and associates (2004) created the 3Di to identify ASD symptoms in either clinical or general populations. They described it as a hybrid that combines the strengths of structured and semi-structured interview formats in order to avoid biased responses from interviewees who may be familiar with the symptoms of particular diagnostic categories. Another advantage of the 3Di is its use of computerized scoring, which lessens time demands on clinicians who might wish to use it (Roth, 2010).

The 3Di contains 183 items that gather information about a person's developmental history and family background, 266 items that pertain to ASD, and 291 items that ask about symptoms relevant to other diagnoses. Items are grouped into modules; those that relate to ASD are mandatory but modules that request information about possible comorbid conditions are optional. An interviewee's responses can be coded on a scale from 0 to 2. A score of 0 means that no such behavior occurs, a score of 1 is given when there is slight evidence of a behavior, and a score of 2 indicates that a behavior is definitely evident or persistent. The complete set of questions about ASD can be completed in approximately 90 minutes. When administering this interview, a clinician must read the questions exactly as they appear on a computer screen and then make notes about the client's responses; these can be coded following the conclusion of the interview. A report that includes detailed information about the interviewee's symptoms can be generated immediately after all responses have been coded (Skuse et al., 2004).

Skuse et al. (2004) conducted analyses to examine the psychometric properties of their instrument and found that the 3Di has excellent test–retest reliability and interrater reliability. They reported that the 3Di demonstrates strong concurrent, criterion, and discriminant validity as well. Because the 3Di can be used with both clinical and nonclinical populations (Skuse et al., 2004), it can be employed as a measure of ASD symptoms that are components of the BAP (e.g., see Mandy et al., 2014, which was described earlier in this chapter).

Interviews that were designed for purposes other than the assessment of ASD sometimes have been used to examine characteristics of the BAP. For example, Piven et al. (1991) chose the Schedule for Affective Disorders and Schizophrenia Lifetime Version (SADS-L; Endicott & Spitzer, 1978; Harrington et al., 1988) to obtain information about prevalence rates of psychiatric disorders in parents of individuals with autism. The SADS-L yields information about lifetime prevalence rates of various categories of psychopathology such as schizophrenia, mood disorders, anxiety disorders, and substance-related disorders, among others (Piven et al., 1991). When compared to parents of people with Down syndrome, parents of autism probands had a significantly higher lifetime prevalence rate of anxiety disorders. Use of the SADS-L in this study also revealed that the lifetime prevalence rate for major depressive disorder was higher than in the general population (Piven et al., 1991). It should be noted, however, that the SADS was developed prior to the third edition of the *DSM*, which was published in 1980 (Mannuzza, Fyer, Klein, & Endicott, 1986). Therefore, it would be difficult (perhaps impossible) to use the SADS-L to obtain *DSM-5* diagnoses of disorders that coexist with the BAP.

2.2.2. Observational Approaches

Pickles et al. (2013a) wrote that the best way to assess the BAP is through the combined use of self-report interviews, interviews with collateral informants, and observation. The Autism Diagnostic Observation Schedule (ADOS; Lord, Rutter, DiLavore, & Risi, 1999) is regarded as a reliable and valid observational method for diagnosing ASD in both children and adults (Bastiaansen et al., 2011). However, it does not provide algorithms or scores for the identification of the BAP.

An instrument that is intended for assessment of the BAP, which consists of both a semi-structured interview and an observational component, is the Broader Phenotype Autism Symptom Scale (BPASS; Dawson et al., 2007). The BPASS should be administered by clinicians with advanced training, such as licensed clinical psychologists or doctoral-level graduate students. Its interview section contains seven questions that a parent can answer, either about his or her own functioning or about the functioning of a child with ASD. These questions ask about such topics as the amount of time spent with other people, level of comfort in social situations, whether a preference for predictability exists, and whether interests interfere with relationships or daily functioning. The observation portion of the BPASS requires the test administrator to rate four domains of BAP characteristics that were apparent during the course of the clinical interview segment. The domain of nonverbal communication includes an evaluation of the interviewee's use of eye contact, vocal prosody, facial expressions, and social smiles. With regard to the domain of social motivation, the clinician rates the extent of the test participant's interactions with peers and comfort in groups. The third domain, conversational skill, is examined in terms of using excessive conversational detail and talking with others in a disorganized or vague manner. Finally, the fourth domain considers the interviewee's flexibility concerning routines and environments (Dawson et al., 2007).

Most BPASS items are rated on 4- or 5-point scales. Four-point items provide symptom ratings that vary from typical functioning (1) to significantly below average functioning (4). Items using a 5-point scale range from above-average functioning (1) to markedly impaired (5). However, observations about the variability of the interviewee's facial expressions employ only a 3-point scale because it was not otherwise possible to obtain sufficient interrater reliability for that item (Dawson et al., 2007). A BPASS score of 1 or 2 on an item denotes typical behavior whereas a score of 3 or higher is viewed as below normal (Gerdts, Bernier, Dawson, & Estes, 2013). Scores also can be calculated for each of the four BPASS domains (Dawson et al., 2007).

Dawson and colleagues (2007) examined the psychometric qualities of the BPASS, using data from 690 people who came from over 200 families in which there were at least 2 children with ASD. Analyses of these data revealed that internal consistencies for the four BPASS domains were good and interrater reliability was adequate. Sung et al. (2005) also reported that the BPASS has acceptable convergent validity with the FHI, although Dawson et al. mentioned that the BPASS and FHI provide slightly different measurements of the BAP when used to evaluate parents of children with ASD. Initial studies using the BPASS suggest that it has potential as a method for quantifying BAP traits (Dawson et al., 2007).

An advantage of the BPASS is that it reduces the possibility of rater bias. Bernier, Gerdts, Munson, Dawson, and Estes (2012) employed the BPASS in a study to examine BAP features in parents of families with multiple children with ASD. They obtained BPASS ratings made by live observers who knew whether parents being interviewed were from simplex or multiplex families. Bernier et al. compared these ratings to the ratings of videotaped interviews which had been given by observers who were naive to the family status of the parents. Their analyses revealed that ratings from live observations were significantly correlated to ratings for videotaped observations. In addition, they found no significant differences in ratings for any of the four domains measured by the BPASS.

Another observational method that is in development to examine the BAP is the Impressions of Interviewee (IoI) measure (Davidson et al., 2012; Pickles et al., 2013a). The IoI consists of 20 items that deal with observable characteristics of the BAP, such as facial expression, use of eye contact, prosody, rigid behavior, irritable mood, repetitive mentions of special interest topics, and so on. A clinician who uses the IoI would first conduct an interview such as the FHI. Then he or she would complete the IoI based on what was observed about the respondent during administration of the clinical interview. Each IoI item receives a rating on a scale from 0 to 2. A rating of 0 indicates that no problems are evident in the BAP trait being observed. A score of 1 means that the person being observed does have difficulty in that particular area, and a score of 2 is given when the person clearly demonstrates the trait (Pickles et al., 2013a). Thus, higher scores suggest the presence of the BAP (Davidson et al., 2012).

Unfortunately, psychometric analyses have shown that the IoI requires modifications before it can be widely used for research or clinical evaluations. Of greatest concern is its relatively low test—retest reliability. Because the BAP involves a set of characteristics that persist over time, the lack of adequate test—retest reliability must be remedied before the IoI is ready for widespread use (Pickles et al., 2013a).

2.2.3. Rating Scales and Questionnaires

A variety of instruments exist for identifying the BAP, some of which are screening measures. Screening tools detect individuals within a general population who may have a clinically relevant condition that might benefit from further assistance (Robins, 2008; Roth, 2010). One such measure that is capable of finding cases of the BAP is the Autism Spectrum Screening Questionnaire (ASSQ; Ehlers & Gillberg, 1993). Although this assessment device initially was created to identify Asperger's disorder in school-aged children, it has been found helpful when screening for other forms of ASD in youngsters (Posserud, Lundervold, & Gillberg, 2009). This 27-item checklist asks the rater (either a parent or teacher) to indicate whether a child who is being screened exhibits problems with communication or difficulty in social exchanges, as well as stereotyped behaviors, physical clumsiness, and vocal or motor tics. ASSQ items are rated on a 3-point scale, with scores of 0 indicating typical development, scores of 1 denoting some degree of abnormality, and scores of 2 signifying the definite presence of a problem. This checklist can be completed in roughly 10 minutes (Ehlers, Gillberg, & Wing, 1999) and has good reliability and validity (Posserud et al., 2009).

Posserud and associates (2009) employed the ASSQ to screen 9,430 Norwegian children from 7 to 9 years of age in the context of a longitudinal research program known as the Bergen Child Study. Parents and teachers completed the ASSQ for this sample. The researchers decided to use ASSQ cutoff scores at the 98th percentile; these were equivalent to scores that exceeded 18 points on ASSQs completed by parents, or that were higher than 15 points on ASSQs from teachers. Using these benchmarks, 212 children screened positive for possible ASD. Follow-up assessments of children who screened positive on the ASSQ involved the administration of structured clinical interviews and other measures to arrive at diagnoses. Based on this process, nine boys were identified as having the BAP, which Posserud et al. defined as demonstrating obvious ASD features yet having symptoms that were either too few or too subtle to warrant a diagnosis of ASD. The authors discovered that seven of these nine boys were identified on the basis of ASSQ reports from teachers but not from parents. In other words, only two children with the BAP in this sample could be identified by using parent ASSQ findings. Posserud et al. speculated that parents may have trouble noticing mild social deficits in their children because the parents themselves might have the BAP. As a result, these investigators concluded that data from not only parents but also teachers should be gathered when using the ASSQ for screening purposes. In addition, they determined that a cutoff score of 17 points or higher was optimal for use with both of these groups of informants.

Population screening to detect the BAP also has been done using the Modified Checklist for Autism in Toddlers (M-CHAT; Robins, Fein, Barton, & Green, 2001). This instrument, which derives from the Checklist for Autism in Toddlers (CHAT; Baron-Cohen, Allen, & Gillberg, 1992), consists of 23 yes/no items, the first nine of which come directly from the CHAT (Robins et al., 2001). Preliminary investigation of the M-CHAT's psychometric properties indicated that its internal consistency, sensitivity, and specificity are adequate. The M-CHAT was designed for use during routine pediatric examinations of toddlers ranging in age from 14 to 30 months old (Robins, 2008; Robins et al., 2001). It is completed by parents, who indicate whether their child demonstrates ASD symptoms such as the child's failure to respond to his or her own name, problems with joint attention, and lack of interest in other children (Robins et al., 2001). A failure on any three or more M-CHAT items, or on any two of its six critical items, suggests that a child is at risk for ASD and should undergo additional evaluation (Robins, 2008).

From March of 2005 through October of 2007, Robins (2008) collected M-CHAT data from nearly 4,800 children in the greater metropolitan area of Atlanta, Georgia. Among them, 466 children screened positive for possible ASD, and 362 of these opted for a follow-up interview. In the interview group, 61 children were referred for further evaluation and 41 of these families agreed to participate in the examination. Four cases in this study that initially were deemed at risk on the basis of their M-CHAT scores eventually were classified as having the BAP. However, two more children who ultimately were classified as cases of the BAP were flagged by their physician as possibly at risk for ASD even though their M-CHAT scores did not signal cause for concern. Thus, although results of the Robins study support the use of the M-CHAT as a screening instrument for ASD in a general population, they also suggest that this measure alone is insufficient to identify the BAP.

Beyond clinical purposes, another reason to screen for the BAP is to search for genes associated with risk for ASD. A measure that often has been used in this manner is the Autism Spectrum Quotient (AQ; Baron-Cohen, Wheelwright, Skinner, Martin, & Clubley, 2001). Baron-Cohen and colleagues (2001) wished to create a self-administered questionnaire for adults of normal intelligence that could quickly and conveniently determine whether the test-taker has the BAP. Versions of the AQ also have been designed for use with children from ages 4 to 11 years old, and for adolescents from 12 to 16 years old (Wheelwright, Auyeung, Allison, & Baron-Cohen, 2010).

The adult AQ is a 50-item assessment containing five scales comprised of 10 items each (Baron-Cohen et al., 2001). However, factor-analytic studies conducted by other researchers (e.g., Austin, 2005; Hoekstra, Bartels, Cath, & Boomsma, 2008; Hurst, Mitchell, Kimbrel, Kwapil, & Nelson-Gray, 2007; Stewart & Austin, 2009) suggest that only two to four latent factors may underlie the AQ, rather than the five scales proposed by its originators. Scales of the AQ inquire about the respondent's social skill, ability to shift attention, attention to detail, communication ability, and imagination. For each item, a respondent indicates definite agreement, slight agreement, slight disagreement, or definite disagreement. To prevent response bias, roughly half of the AQ items were phrased to elicit disagreement, and the remaining items were worded in the direction of agreement. An item receives a score of 1 if the test-taker endorses an ASD trait, whether mildly or strongly. Thus, points are assigned for answers indicating deficits in social skill, communication, and imagination, as well as responses denoting unusual attention to detail, problems in switching attention, or excessive focus on a topic. Scores on the AQ may vary from 0 to 50, thereby providing a quantitative measure regarding where a person lies on the ASD continuum. Preliminary examination of the AQ's psychometric properties revealed adequate internal consistency, good test—retest reliability, and good interrater reliability (Baron-Cohen et al., 2001).

Originally written in English, the AQ has been employed by researchers in Great Britain (Austin, 2005; Wheelwright et al., 2010), Scotland (Stewart & Austin, 2009), Israel (Milshtein, Yirmiya, Oppenheim, Koren-Karie, & Levi, 2010), and the United States (Hurst et al., 2007; Wainer, Ingersoll, & Hopwood, 2011). It also has been translated into French (Robel et al., 2014), Dutch (Hoekstra et al., 2008; Poljac, Poljac, & Yeung, 2012; Scheeren & Stauder, 2008), Italian (Ruta, Mazzone, Mazzone, Wheelwright, & Baron-Cohen, 2012), Persian (Mohammadi, Zarafshan, & Ghasempour, 2012), and Turkish (Kose et al., 2013).

Several studies have utilized the AQ to investigate the BAP. For example, Bishop et al. (2004) gave the AQ to parents of 69 people with ASD and parents of 52 control individuals. They discovered that two AQ scales (i.e., social skills and communication) distinguished between the two groups of parents, with ASD parents having higher scores on these scales. In this study 17 fathers and 10 mothers were found to have the BAP. Interestingly, these individuals did not differ from controls in verbal intelligence as measured by a short form of the Wechsler Adult Intelligence Scale, even though they did achieve high scores on the AQ communication scale (Bishop et al., 2004).

Wheelwright et al. (2010) also used the AQ to examine the parameters of the narrow, medium, and broad autism phenotypes in parents of children with ASD. They administered the AQ to 571 fathers and 1,429 mothers of children with ASD, in addition to 349 fathers and 658 mothers of neurotypical children. Wheelwright and colleagues operationally defined the BAP as an AQ score of 23–28 points, which was 1–2 standard deviations above the AQ mean score of all control parents in this study. Similarly, they defined the medium autism phenotype (MAP) as AQ scores of 29–34, which was equivalent to 2–3 standard deviations above the mean. The narrow autism phenotype (NAP) was defined as having an AQ score greater than or equal to 35 points (i.e., 3 or more standard deviations above the mean of the control group). Results demonstrated that parents of ASD children scored higher than parents of typically developing children on the total AQ score and on four of the five AQ scales. Among the parents of ASD children in this study, 33% of fathers and 23% of mothers met or exceeded the AQ cutoff for the BAP. Also, in comparison to control parents, significantly more ASD parents obtained scores in the range of the MAP or NAP. On the basis of these outcomes, Wheelwright et al. declared,

"The AQ is thus a reasonable tool for assessing whether individuals can be classified as having the BAP" (p. 5).

Wainer et al. (2011) included the AQ when investigating the BAP in two large, nonclinical samples of undergraduate university students. They performed an exploratory factor analysis (EFA) of the AQ and obtained five factors that resembled its five scales. However, when including two other BAP measures together with the AQ in a conjoint EFA, these authors determined that only three factors were necessary to describe the BAP: pragmatic language deficits, aloofness, and rigidity. Thus, while the AQ can be used to identify the BAP, not all researchers seem to agree with its conceptualization of the components that make up the BAP.

Another instrument called the Children's Communication Checklist-2 (CCC-2; Bishop, 2003) can be used to screen siblings of children with ASD. It was designed for administration to children in the age range of 4–16 years old. The CCC-2 consists of ten 7-item scales, four of which examine the structural language characteristics of speech, syntax, semantics, and coherence. Four other scales assess pragmatic language abilities such as initiation of conversation and the use of stereotyped language, context, and nonverbal communication. The remaining two scales investigate social relations and the interests of the child being evaluated, both of which relate directly to ASD. Each CCC-2 scale contains five items that ask about weaknesses and two items that inquire about strengths. A parent completes this checklist by rating the frequency with which each item is observed, ranging from 0 (less than once a week, to never) up to 3 (more than twice a day, to always). The score on each subscale is converted to an age-scaled score that has a mean of 10 and a standard deviation of 3. The CCC-2 also yields two composite scores. The first is a General Communication Composite (GCC) that results from adding the first eight scales. The second is the Social Interaction Deviance Composite (SIDC). It is calculated by adding the scale scores for inappropriate initiation, nonverbal communication, social relations, and interests, and then subtracting the scores for speech, syntax, semantics, and coherence. The resulting SIDC provides a way to gauge the disparity between structural and pragmatic language skills (Bishop, Maybery, Wong, Maley, & Hallmayer, 2006).

When Bishop and colleagues (2006) employed the CCC-2 with a group of 43 siblings of ASD probands, they found 10 children whose scores signified communication problems but who did not meet criteria to be diagnosed with ASD. Furthermore, five fathers of these children fit the definition of the BAP. These researchers noted that it is much easier and quicker to administer a CCC-2 rather than a diagnostic interview, and they surmised that subtle difficulties with social communication may run in families.

An adult version of the CCC-2 exists in the form of the Communication Checklist-Adult (CC-A; Whitehouse & Bishop, 2009). Factor analyses of data obtained from a standardization sample revealed that this assessment contains three scales which the authors labeled Language Structure, Pragmatic Skills, and Social Engagement (Whitehouse, Coon, Miller, Salisbury, & Bishop, 2010). Like the CCC-2, the CC-A contains 70 items that are rated on the same scale of 0–3; however, the content of these items was adjusted to apply to adults. The checklist is completed by someone who is highly familiar with the person being evaluated. Like the CCC-2, scores for each scale of the CC-A have been standardized to have a mean score of 10 and a standard deviation of 3. However, sex differences were noted, with males tending to score lower than females on the Pragmatic Skills and Social Engagement scales. For this reason, Whitehouse and associates (2010) created gender-specific standard scores for these two scales. They also created a CC-A total score by adding the raw scores for all 70 items and then adjusting for sex differences by converting to separate z-scores for men and for women.

Using the CC-A to evaluate parents of ASD index cases, Whitehouse et al. (2010) found that 13% of their ASD parent sample showed significant problems in comparison to 8% of participants in a neurotypical control group. In this study, most of the parents who manifested the BAP obtained poor scores on either the Pragmatic Skills scale or the Social Engagement scale but not on both scales. These findings contrasted with CC-A results for adults with ASD; more than two-thirds of ASD participants yielded poor scores on both of the aforementioned scales. Thus, Whitehouse et al. expressed a belief that different communication profiles can be found within the BAP. In particular, they noted that pragmatic language difficulties are much more likely than structural language deficits. Whitehouse and associates also suggested that by using the CC-A, scientists who are interested in molecular genetic studies of ASD can quickly identify participants for genetic research.

Similarly, a measure known as the Social Responsiveness Scale (SRS; Constantino, 2002) can be employed to facilitate genetic research concerning ASD and the BAP (e.g., see Maxwell, Parish-Morris, Hsin, Bush, & Schultz, 2013). This instrument, formerly called the Social Reciprocity Scale, consists of 65 items that can be completed in approximately 15–20 minutes. Parents or teachers rate a child's difficulties in relation to social awareness, social information processing, pragmatic language, capacity for social responses, preoccupations, and repetitive behaviors. These items are scored on a scale from 0, which represents "never true," to 3, which indicates "almost always true" (Constantino et al., 2004, p. 721). The SRS produces a single score, with higher scores denoting more severe social dysfunction (Constantino et al., 2004).

An adult version of this measure, the Social Responsiveness Scale-Adult (SRS-A; Constantino & Todd, 2005), also was developed. Some researchers have referred to this same instrument as the Social Responsiveness Scale: Adult Research Version (SRS: ARV), and state that it should be completed by the spouse or partner of the adult being rated (Davidson et al., 2012). However, Wainer et al. (2011) claimed that the SRS-A can be used as a self-report by instructing a respondent to indicate how others would describe his or her behavior. Upon completion, the SRS-A yields a T score that can be compared to standardized norms. A T score of 70 or higher is equal to two or more standard deviations above the mean and is deemed to be clinically significant (Davidson et al., 2012).

Individuals from a multiple-site sample known as the Simons Simplex Collection served as participants in Davidson et al.'s (2012) research on the BAP. This sample is made up of families in which there is only one child with ASD, and none of the child's first-, second-, or third-degree relatives are thought to have ASD. Davidson and associates gathered SRS-A data from nearly 3,300 parents of children with ASD. Among them, 87 women and 120 men surpassed the cutoff score on the SRS-A. Gender differences were noted, with women scoring significantly higher than men on the Cognition and Mannerisms subscales of the SRS-A and men scoring significantly higher than women on the SRS-A scales measuring Awareness, Communication, and Motivation. However, Davidson et al. noted that most parents in their study did not evince the BAP, which aligned with other studies that also found low rates of the BAP in simplex families (e.g., Losh et al., 2008).

When Wainer and colleagues (2011) performed an EFA on SRS-A data, they identified three latent factors that they called social eccentricity, interpersonal awareness, and social avoidance. In contrast, Davidson et al. (2012) asserted that the SRS-A defines the BAP as a single construct comprised only of social impairment. These disparities highlight current differences in the way that researchers define the key elements of the BAP. Furthermore, as Davidson and colleagues observed, the rate of the BAP in a sample may vary markedly on the basis of the BAP assessment measure being used.

Recently, the author of the original SRS created a revised second edition (SRS-2; Constantino, 2012) so that the instrument would be more compatible with *DSM-5*. This newer measure is available in parent and teacher report forms for preschoolers aged 2.5 through 4.5 years, and for school-aged children and adolescents from ages 4 through 18 years. Separate norms are available for males and females, and an adult self-report version of the SRS-2 also exists.

Yet another measure that was developed for evaluating adults is the Broad Autism Phenotype Questionnaire (BAPQ; Hurley, Losh, Parlier, Reznick, & Piven, 2007). Hurley and colleagues (2007) assembled a self-report measure of characteristics that they believed to be most germane to the BAP: aloofness, rigidity, and pragmatic language impairment. The investigators chose these three characteristics on the basis of previous research findings. Also, these features corresponded well with domains of ASD as listed in the fourth edition of the *DSM*, namely relationship deficits, repetitive behaviors, and problems in social communication. Hurley et al. conducted two pilot studies with convenience samples to examine potential questionnaire items for their utility, and eliminated items that did not reflect the three traits deemed most relevant to the BAP. The resulting instrument consisted of three 12-item subscales that reflected BAP traits but were seldom endorsed by respondents in the pilot samples. Next, the BAPQ was given to 86 parents of children with autism, with 64 parents of neurotypical children serving as controls. To reduce the likelihood of response bias, respondents were told that the measure was called the Personality Styles and Preferences Questionnaire. These individuals were asked to rate themselves concerning how often each item pertained to them. Additionally, they were instructed to rate themselves according to their typical manner of interaction with most people for the duration of their adult lives, and to guess on items of which they were unsure. Not only did participants rate themselves, but most of them also completed an informant version of the BAPQ about their spouse or partner (Hurley et al., 2007).

BAPQ items are scored on a scale from 1 to 6, with a score of 1 signaling that the item applied very rarely and a score of 6 indicating that the item applied very often. To further guard against response bias, some items are reverse scored. Item scores for each BAPQ scale are averaged to provide subscale scores that range from 1 to 6. In like fashion, all BAPQ items are averaged to yield a total score. Statistical analyses of the three BAPQ scales produced high internal consistencies for all three subscales and for the 36-item instrument as a whole. Furthermore, correlations between subscales were similar for male and female participants, as well as when comparing self-reports versus informant reports (Hurley et al., 2007).

To validate the BAPQ, Hurley et al. (2007) conducted in-person clinical interviews with ASD parents, using the M-PAS-R (previously discussed in this chapter) and the Pragmatic Rating Scale (PRS; Landa et al., 1992). Interviewees were asked about themselves and about their spouses or partners. The interviews were videotaped and later coded by expert raters to identify which parents met criteria for the BAP. Direct assessment of the BAP via these interviews located 22 ASD parents who had the BAP. When comparing this number against predictions based on the BAPQ total score, the BAPQ demonstrated sensitivity and specificity that exceeded 70%. Sensitivity describes an instrument's ability to correctly identify actual cases of the BAP, and specificity involves the ability to correctly classify respondents who do not have the BAP. Sensitivity and specificity above 70% is desirable. Parents of ASD children scored significantly higher than control parents on all three subscales of the BAPQ. Thus, on the basis of their results and psychometric calculations, Hurley et al. stated the BAPQ "provides a valid and efficient measure for characterizing the BAP" (p. 1679).

Sugihara, Tsuchiya, and Takei (2008), however, raised concerns that people with schizophrenia and related conditions (e.g., schizoid and schizotypal personality disorders) might be misclassified as having the BAP if only the BAPQ were used for assessment. These authors reported that they had administered the BAPQ to three people on the schizophrenia spectrum, all of whom obtained BAPQ scores that were higher than the recommended BAPQ cutoff scores. Therefore, Sugihara and colleagues suggested that the BAPQ should be modified by adding items that would help to distinguish respondents with schizophrenia and related conditions from those with the BAP. In response, the authors of the BAPQ clarified that they intended for their instrument to be used as a screening measure rather than a standalone assessment device (see Piven, Hurley, Losh, Parlier, & Reznick, 2008). They wrote, "... we are less certain about its use as a diagnostic tool" (Piven et al., 2008, p. 2000) and voiced agreement with Sugihara et al. (2008) regarding the need to fine-tune the BAPQ's specificity.

In an effort to improve this psychometric aspect of the BAPQ, Sasson et al. (2013a) conducted a study in which data were gathered from a much larger sample than the one with which the BAPQ was developed. Participants included 711 parents of ASD children, 12% of whom reported having more than one child with ASD. They completed the BAPQ self-report as well as an informant report about their partner or spouse. A subset of 35 parents of ASD children underwent further clinical evaluation using the M-PAS-R (previously discussed) and the Modified Pragmatic Rating Scale (MPRS). The latter instrument, derived from the PRS (Landa et al., 1992) was used to detect pragmatic language abilities and grammatical errors. Sasson and colleagues also recruited 981 community-dwelling adults to serve as a comparison group in which the rate of BAP traits could be examined in a general population. Sasson et al. found that rates of the BAP ranged from 14% to 23% in parents of children with ASD, while the BAP was identified in only 5–9% of their comparison group. Results of this investigation led to the establishment of new cutoff scores for the BAPQ that improved its specificity and made it more useful for identifying the BAP. Despite this improvement, Sasson and associates recommended that the cutoff scores initially selected by Hurley et al. (2007) should continue to be used during screenings because the original cutoffs provide greater sensitivity regarding identification of the BAP.

A study by Ingersoll, Hopwood, Wainer, and Donnellan (2011) compared the BAPQ with the SRS-A and the AQ, examining these three instruments' distribution of scores, internal consistency, factor structure, and criterion validity. For all three assessment measures, total scores and subscale scores formed continuous distributions. Internal consistencies for each measure were acceptable, although both the BAPQ and the SRS-A had better internal consistencies than the AQ. An EFA of the SRS-A suggested that three or four factors were present, rather than only a single factor as had been posited by its authors. Separate EFAs of the AQ and BAPQ indicated three factors per instrument, yet the BAPQ's factor loadings were most consistent with the three-factor structure that had been described by its creators. This finding was later corroborated by an EFA done within the context of the Sasson et al. (2013a) investigation, which also yielded three latent factors that aligned with the proposed constructs of aloofness, pragmatic language, and rigidity.

Correlational analyses performed by Ingersoll et al. (2011) found that the BAPQ, SRS-A, and AQ correlated strongly with one another, demonstrating that all three of them are evaluating the same construct. However, criterion validity of the AQ was not as strong as for the BAPQ or SRS-A, which Ingersoll and colleagues attributed to the AQ's weaker internal consistency. As a result, they recommended that the BAPQ and SRS-A are preferable to the AQ when measuring the BAP. In fact, according to Ingersoll et al., the BAPQ is the best of these three instruments for identifying the BAP. They pointed out that only the BAPQ was designed specifically for the purpose of assessing the BAP, whereas the other two measures were devised to measure ASD. Another advantage of the BAPQ is its brevity in comparison to its two alternatives (Ingersoll et al., 2011).

Other studies that have employed the BAPQ include Maxwell et al. (2013), Sasson, Lam, Parlier, Daniels, and Piven (2013b), and Seidman, Yirmiya, Milshtein, Ebstein, and Levi (2012). The second of these investigations will be discussed further in Chapter 3.

An assessment device that may have potential for identifying the BAP in an adult general population is the Subthreshold Autism Trait Questionnaire (SATQ; Kanne, Wang, & Christ, 2012). Kanne and colleagues created a self-report instrument that could quickly and easily measure ASD traits. Furthermore, they chose to devise the SATQ so that it could be employed not only with people suspected of having ASD and their relatives, but also with a non-ASD population. Their rationale for doing so came from research findings that ASD traits exist as a continuous distribution throughout the general population (Constantino, 2011). Such traits will be most evident in people who are diagnosed with ASD but also will appear to a lesser extent in their non-ASD relatives, some of whom might be labeled more properly as having the BAP (Kanne et al., 2012).

During the development of the SATQ, a large sample of undergraduate students at a Midwestern public university took an initial version of the questionnaire. In addition, a small group of adults in the community who had a diagnosis of ASD were recruited for this purpose. Participants completed an initial pool of 32 items, responding to each on a 4-point scale. Some items were worded so that high scores would indicate ASD traits, while others were scored in the opposite direction to protect against response bias (Kanne et al., 2012). Upon conducting an item distribution analysis and examining item-total correlations, Kanne et al. (2012) removed eight items from their preliminary pool of questions. The revised SATQ then consisted of 24 items which demonstrated good internal consistency, test–retest reliability, and convergent validity with other measures of ASD. Exploratory and confirmatory analyses yielded five SATQ subscales: "Social Interaction and Enjoyment, Oddness, Reading Facial Expressions, Expressive Language, and Rigidity" (Kanne et al., 2012, p. 779).

According to Kanne and colleagues (2012), the SATQ measures some features of the BAP that may not be included in other ASD assessments. These authors reported that the SATQ includes questions about shared enjoyment, expressive language, unusual behaviors and gestures, eye contact, and empathy, all of which may not be well captured by other self-reports. However, Kanne et al. cautioned that because their instrument was developed using a nonclinical sample, further studies are necessary before the SATQ can be utilized for either screening or diagnostic purposes. Also, because the SATQ was developed using data from adult respondents, it is not yet known whether this instrument can be employed to screen children for the BAP.

Similar to the study by Ingersoll et al. (2011), Nishiyama et al. (2014) included the SATQ with the BAPQ, the AQ, and the adult version of the SRS-2 (SRS2-A) in a study to examine the reliability and validity of these instruments. Short forms of the AQ and SRS2-A also were analyzed in regard to their psychometric properties. More than 3,000 people from a general population, as well as 60 individuals with ASD, participated in this research. All participants were adults of normal intelligence. While test−retest reliability was found to be sufficient for all of the measures in this study, short forms of the AQ had poor internal consistency. Furthermore, the AQ and the SRS2-A scores demonstrated poor discriminant validity. Nishiyama and colleagues concluded that the SATQ was preferable to the other assessment devices in their study for measuring quantitative ASD traits, due to its better psychometric characteristics as well as its brief length.

Two of the BAPQ's authors (Piven & Sasson, 2014) took exception to the inclusion of the BAPQ in the Nishiyama et al. (2014) investigation. Piven and Sasson (2014) wrote that the BAPQ is intended specifically for the identification of the BAP, rather than as a measure of quantitative ASD traits. They also expressed concern that the BAPQ is not appropriate for administration to people who have been diagnosed with ASD, as had been done by Nishiyama et al. Additionally, Piven and Sasson claimed that although the BAP may involve milder forms of ASD traits, in other respects it qualitatively differs from ASD. In particular, Piven and Sasson (2014) asserted that the BAPQ measures the characteristic of rigidity, which they defined as a preference for routine. These authors distinguished rigidity from the repetitive behaviors that are found in ASD. They further noted that the BAP does not include functional impairment, and they wondered whether individuals with ASD would be capable of responding appropriately to the BAPQ because such persons might have language impairments. In response, Nishiyama and Kanne (2014) justified administering the BAPQ to adults with ASD because doing so allowed them to examine the construct validity of the instrument. Nishiyama and Kanne also noted that like the BAPQ, some of the other measures in their earlier study also did not contain items that directly measure repetitive behaviors. Finally, they thought it desirable for the BAPQ to be capable of measuring autistic traits in people with ASD, despite such respondents' potential problems with the linguistic nuances of self-reports.

As is evident from the information discussed in this chapter, those who seek to identify the BAP for either investigative or clinical purposes would do well to keep in mind that "… it may be arbitrary where a line is drawn between the condition of being affected versus unaffected by autism" (Constantino, 2011, p. 515). Research has demonstrated that ASD traits can be found and measured even in nonclinical populations. Therefore, detection of the BAP can be challenging due to the lack of uniformity in the way that clinicians and scientists define it, as well as the differing ways that it manifests in males versus females. Also, different assessment devices emphasize different aspects of the BAP. Thus, optimal assessment of the BAP should incorporate self-reports, information from multiple informants, and direct clinical observation (Davidson et al., 2012).

REFERENCES

American Psychiatric Association (APA). (2013). *Diagnostic and statistical manual of mental disorders* (5th ed./*DSM-5*). Washington, DC: Author.

Austin, E. J. (2005). Personality correlates of the broader autism phenotype as assessed by the Autism Spectrum Quotient (AQ). *Personality and Individual Differences, 38*(2), 451–460. doi:10.1016/j.paid.2004.04.022

Baron-Cohen, S., Allen, J., & Gillberg, C. (1992). Can autism be detected at 18 months? The needle, the haystack, and the CHAT. *British Journal of Psychiatry, 161*, 839–843. doi:10.1192/bjp.161.6.839

Baron-Cohen, S., Wheelwright, S., Skinner, R., Martin, J., & Clubley, E. (2001). The Autism Spectrum Quotient (AQ): Evidence from Asperger syndrome/high-functioning autism, males and females, scientists and mathematicians. *Journal of Autism and Developmental Disorders, 31*(1), 5–17. doi:10.1023/A:1005653411471

Bastiaansen, J. A., Meffert, H., Hein, S., Huizinga, P., Ketelaars, C., Pijnenborg, M., … de Bildt, A. (2011). Diagnosing autism spectrum disorders in adults: The use of Autism Diagnostic Observation Schedule (ADOS) module 4. *Journal of Autism and Developmental Disorders, 41*(9), 1256–1266. doi:10.1007/s10803-010-1157-x

Bernier, R., Gerdts, J., Munson, J., Dawson, G., & Estes, A. (2012). Evidence for broader autism phenotype characteristics in parents from multiple incidence autism families. *Autism Research, 5*(1), 13–20. doi:10.1002/aur.226

Bishop, D. V. M. (2003). *The Children's Communication Checklist, version 2 (CCC-2)*. London: Psychological Corporation.

Bishop, D. V. M., Maybery, M., Maley, A., Wong, D., Hill, W., & Hallmayer, J. (2004). Using self-report to identify the broad phenotype in parents of children with autistic spectrum disorders: A study using the Autism-Spectrum Quotient. *Journal of Child Psychology and Psychiatry, 45*(8), 1431–1436. doi:10.1111/j.1469-7610.2004.00325.x

Bishop, D. V. M., Maybery, M., Wong, D., Maley, A., & Hallmayer, J. (2006). Characteristics of the broader phenotype in autism: A study of siblings using the Children's Communication Checklist-2. *American Journal of Medical Genetics Part B (Neuropsychiatric Genetics)*, *141B*, 117–122. doi:10.1002/ajmg.b.30267

Bolton, P., Macdonald, H., Pickles, A., Rios, P., Goode, S., Crowson, M., ... Rutter, M. (1994). A case-control family history study of autism. *Journal of Child Psychology and Psychiatry*, *35*(5), 877–900. doi:10.1111/j.1469-7610.1994.tb02300.x

Buxbaum, J. D., & Baron-Cohen, S. (2013). DSM-5: The debate continues. *Molecular Autism*, *4*(11). doi:10.1186/2040-2392-4-11

Constantino, J. N. (2002). *The social responsiveness scale*. Los Angeles, CA: Western Psychological Services.

Constantino, J. N. (2011). Autism as a quantitative trait. In D. G. Amaral, G. Dawson, & D. H. Geschwind (Eds.), *Autism spectrum disorders* (pp. 510–520). New York, NY: Oxford University Press, Inc.

Constantino, J. N. (2012). *Social responsiveness scale* (2nd ed., SRS-2). Los Angeles, CA: Western Psychological Services.

Constantino, J. N., Gruber, C. P., Davis, S., Hayes, S., Passanante, N., & Przybeck, T. (2004). The factor structure of autistic traits. *Journal of Child Psychology and Psychiatry*, *45*(4), 719–726. doi:10.1111/j.1469-7610.2004.00266.x

Constantino, J. N., & Todd, R. D. (2005). Intergenerational transmission of subthreshold autistic traits in the general population. *Biological Psychiatry*, *57*(6), 655–660. doi:10.1016/j.biopsych.2004.12.014

Davidson, J., Goin-Kochel, R. P., Green-Snyder, L. A., Hundley, R. J., Warren, Z., & Peters, S. U. (2012). Expression of the broad autism phenotype in simplex autism families from the Simons Simplex Collection. *Journal of Autism and Developmental Disorders*. (Online publication). doi:10.1007/s10803-012-1492-1

Dawson, G., Estes, A., Munson, J., Schellenberg, G., Bernier, R., & Abbott, R. (2007). Quantitative assessment of autism symptom-related traits in probands and parents: Broader phenotype autism symptom scale. *Journal of Autism and Developmental Disorders*, *37*(3), 523–536. doi:10.1007/s10803-006-0182-2

Duku, E., Szatmari, P., Vaillancourt, T., Georgiades, S., Thompson, A., Liu, X.-Q., ... Bennett, T. (2013). Measurement equivalence of the autism symptom phenotype in children and youth. *Journal of Child Psychology and Psychiatry*, *54*(12), 1346–1355. doi:10.1111/jcpp.12103

Ehlers, S., & Gillberg, C. (1993). The epidemiology of Asperger syndrome: A total population study. *Journal of Child Psychology and Psychiatry and Allied Disciplines*, *34*(8), 1327–1350. doi:10.1111/j.1469-7610.1993.tb0294.x

Ehlers, S., Gillberg, C., & Wing, L. (1999). A screening questionnaire for Asperger syndrome and other high-functioning autism spectrum disorders in school age children. *Journal of Autism and Developmental Disorders*, *29*(2), 129–141. doi:10.1023/A:1023040610384

Endicott, J., & Spitzer, L. R. (1978). A diagnostic interview: The Schedule for Affective Disorders and Schizophrenia. *Archives of General Psychiatry*, *35*(7), 837–844. doi:10.1001/archpsyc.1978.01770310043002

Folstein, S. E., Santangelo, S. L., Gilman, S. E., Piven, J., Landa, R., Lainhart, J., ... Wrozek, M. (1999). Predictors of cognitive test patterns in autism families. *Journal of Child Psychology and Psychiatry*, *40*(7), 1117–1128. doi:10.1111/1469-7610.00528

Fombonne, E., Bolton, P., Prior, J., Jordan, H., & Rutter, M. (1997). A family study of autism: Cognitive patterns and levels in parents and siblings. *Journal of Child Psychology and Psychiatry, 38*(6), 667–683. doi:10.1111/j.1469-7610.1997.tb01694.x

Georgiades, S., Szatmari, P., Boyle, M., Hanna, S., Duku, E., Zwaigenbaum, L., ... Pathways in ASD Study Team. (2013). Investigating phenotypic heterogeneity in children with autism spectrum disorder: A factor mixture modeling approach. *Journal of Child Psychology and Psychiatry, 54*(2), 206–215. doi:10.1111/j.1469-7610.2012.02588.x

Gerdts, J., & Bernier, R. (2011). The broader autism phenotype and its implications on the etiology and treatment of autism spectrum disorders. *Autism Research and Treatment*. Article ID 545901. doi:10.1155/2011/545901

Gerdts, J. A., Bernier, R., Dawson, G., & Estes, A. (2013). The broad autism phenotype in simplex and multiplex families. *Journal of Autism and Developmental Disorders, 43*(7), 1595–1607. doi:10.1007/s10803-012-1706-6

Harrington, R., Hill, J., Rutter, M., John, K., Fudge, H., Zoccolillo, M., & Weissman, M. (1988). The assessment of lifetime psychopathology: A comparison of two interviewing styles. *Psychological Medicine, 18*(2), 487–493. doi:10.1017/S0033291700008023

Hoekstra, R. A., Bartels, M., Cath, D. C., & Boomsma, D. I. (2008). Factor structure, reliability and criterion validity of the Autism-Spectrum Quotient (AQ): A study in Dutch population and patient groups. *Journal of Autism and Developmental Disorders, 38*(8), 1555–1566. doi:10.1007/s10803-008-0538-x

Hurley, R. S. E., Losh, M., Parlier, M., Reznick, J. S., & Piven, J. (2007). The Broad Autism Phenotype Questionnaire. *Journal of Autism and Developmental Disorders, 37*(9), 1679–1690. doi:10.1007/s10803-006-0299-3

Hurst, R. M., Mitchell, J. T., Kimbrel, N. A., Kwapil, T. K., & Nelson-Gray, R. O. (2007). Examination of the reliability and factor structure of the Autism Spectrum Quotient (AQ) in a non-clinical sample. *Personality and Individual Differences, 43*(7), 1938–1949. doi:10.1016/j.paid.2007.06.012

Ingersoll, B., Hopwood, C. J., Wainer, A., & Donnellan, M. B. (2011). A comparison of three self-report measures of the broader autism phenotype in a non-clinical sample. *Journal of Autism and Developmental Disorders, 41*(12), 1646–1657. doi:10.1007/s10803-011-1192-2

Kanne, S. M., Wang, J., & Christ, S. E. (2012). The Subthreshold Autism Trait Questionnaire (SATQ): Development of a brief self-report measure of subthreshold autism traits. *Journal of Autism and Developmental Disorders, 42*(5), 769–780. doi:10.1007/s10803-011-1308-8

Kose, S., Bora, E., Eremis, S., Ozbaran, B., Bildik, T., & Aydin, C. (2013). Broader autistic phenotype in parents of children with autism: Autism Spectrum Quotient-Turkish version. *Psychiatry and Clinical Neurosciences, 67*(1), 20–27. doi:10.1111/pcn.12005

Lai, M.-C., Lombardo, M. V., Chakrabarti, B., & Baron-Cohen, S. (2013). Subgrouping the autism "spectrum": Reflections on DSM-5. *PLoS Biology, 11*(4), e1001544. (Open access article). doi:10.1371/journal.pbio.1001544

Lainhart, J. E., Ozonoff, S., Coon, H., Krasny, L., Dinh, E., Nice, J., & McMahon, W. (2002). Autism, regression, and the broader autism phenotype. *American Journal of Medical Genetics, 113*(3), 231–237. doi:10.1002/ajmg.10615

Landa, R., Piven, J., Wrozek, M. M., Gayle, J. O., Chase, G. A., & Folstein, S. E. (1992). Social language use in parents of autistic individuals. *Psychological Medicine, 22*(1), 245–254. doi:10.1017/S0033291700032918

Le Couteur, A., Bailey, A., Goode, S., Pickles, A., Robertson, S., Gottesman, I., & Rutter, M. (1996). A broader phenotype of autism: The clinical spectrum in twins. *Journal of Child Psychology and Psychiatry, 37*(7), 785–801. doi:10.1111/j.1469-7610.1996.tb01475.x

Le Couteur, A., Rutter, M., Lord, C., Rios, P., Robertson, S., Holdgrafer, M., & McLannen, J. (1989). Autism diagnostic interview: A standardized investigator-based instrument. *Journal of Autism and Developmental Disorders, 19*(3), 363–387. doi:10.1007/BF02212936

Lord, C., Petkova, E., Hus, V., Gan, W., Lu, F., Martin, D. M., ... Risi, S. (2012). A multisite study of the clinical diagnosis of different autism spectrum disorders. *Archives of General Psychiatry, 69*(3), 306–313. doi:10.1001/archgenpsychiatry.2011.148

Lord, C., Rutter, M., DiLavore, P., & Risi, S. (1999). *Autism diagnostic observation schedule: Manual*. Los Angeles, CA: Western Psychological Services.

Lord, C., Rutter, M., & Le Couteur, A. (1994). Autism Diagnostic Interview-Revised: A revised version of a diagnostic interview for caregivers of individuals with possible pervasive developmental disorders. *Journal of Autism and Developmental Disorders, 24*(5), 659–685. doi:10.1007/BF02172145

Losh, M., Adolphs, R., & Piven, J. (2011). The broad autism phenotype. In D. G. Amaral, G. Dawson, & D. H. Geschwind (Eds.), *Autism spectrum disorders* (pp. 457–476). New York, NY: Oxford University Press, Inc.

Losh, M., Adophs, R., Poe, M. D., Couture, S., Penn, D., Baranek, G., & Piven, J. (2009). Neuropsychological profile of autism and the broad autism phenotype. *Archives of General Psychiatry, 66*(5), 518–526. doi:10.1001/archgenpsychiatry.2009.34

Losh, M., Childress, D., Lam, K., & Piven, J. (2008). Defining key features of the broad autism phenotype: A comparison across parents of multiple- and single-incidence autism families. *American Journal of Medical Genetics Part B: Neuropsychiatric Genetics, 147B*(4), 424–433. doi:10.1002/ajmg.b.30612

Losh, M., Esserman, D., & Piven, J. (2010). Rapid automatized naming as an index of genetic liability to autism. *Journal of Neurodevelopmental Disorders, 2*(2), 109–116. doi:10.1007/s11689-010-9045-4

Mandy, W., Charman, T., Puura, K., & Skuse, D. H. (2014). Investigating the cross-cultural validity of *DSM-5* autism spectrum disorder: Evidence from Finnish and UK samples. *Autism, 18*(1), 45–54. doi:10.1177/1362361313508026

Mannuzza, S., Fyer, A. J., Klein, D. F., & Endicott, J. (1986). Schedule for Affective Disorders and Schizophrenia-Lifetime Version modified for the study of anxiety disorders (SADS-LA): Rationale and conceptual development. *Journal of Psychiatric Research, 20*(4), 317–325. doi:10.1016/0022-3956(86)90034-8

Maxwell, C. R., Parish-Morris, J., Hsin, O., Bush, J. C., & Schultz, R. T. (2013). The broad autism phenotype predicts child functioning in autism spectrum disorders. *Journal of Neurodevelopmental Disorders, 5*(1), 25–31. (Open access article). doi:10.1186/1866-1955-5-25

Mazefsky, C. A., Williams, D. L., & Minshew, N. J. (2008). Variability in adaptive behavior in autism: Evidence for the importance of family history. *Journal of Abnormal Child Psychology, 36*(4), 591–599. doi:10.1007/s10802-007-9202-8

Milshtein, S., Yirmiya, N., Oppenheim, D., Koren-Karie, N., & Levi, S. (2010). Resolution of the diagnosis among parents of children with autism spectrum disorder: Associations with child and parent characteristics. *Journal of Autism and Developmental Disorders, 40*(1), 89–99. doi:10.1007/s10803-009-0837-x

Mohammadi, M. R., Zarafshan, H., & Ghasempour, S. (2012). Broader autism phenotype in Iranian parents of children with autism spectrum disorders vs. normal children. *Iranian Journal of Psychiatry*, 7(4), 157−163.

Ne'eman, A., & Kapp, S. (2012, June). What are the stakes? An analysis of the impact of the DSM-5 draft autism criteria on law, policy and service provision. Autistic Self Advocacy Network. Retrieved from http://autisticadvocacy.org/wp-content/uploads/2012/06/DSM-5_Policy_Brief_ASAN_final.pdf

Nishiyama, T., & Kanne, S. M. (2014). On the misapplication of the BAPQ in a study of autism. *Journal of Autism and Developmental Disorders*, 44(8), 2079−2080. doi:10.1007/s10803-014-2077-y

Nishiyama, T., Suzuki, M., Adachi, K., Sumi, S., Okaa, K., Kishino, H., ... Kanne, S. M. (2014). Comprehensive comparison of self-administered questionnaires for measuring quantitative autistic traits in adults. *Journal of Autism and Developmental Disorders*, 44(5), 993−1007. doi:10.1007/s10803-013-2020-7

Pickles, A., Parr, J. R., Rutter, M. L., De Jonge, M. V., Wallace, S., Le Couteur, A. S., ... Bailey, A. J. (2013a). New interview and observation measures of the broader autism phenotype: Impressions of interviewee measure. *Journal of Autism and Developmental Disorders*, 43(9), 2082−2089. doi:10.1007/s10803-013-1810-2

Pickles, A., St. Clair, M. C., & Conti-Ramsden, G. (2013b). Communication and social deficits in relatives of individuals with SLI and relatives of individuals with ASD. *Journal of Autism and Developmental Disorders*, 43(1), 156−167. doi:10.1007/s10803-012-1556-2

Piven, J., Chase, G. A., Landa, R., Wrozek, M., Gayle, J., Cloud, D., & Folstein, S. (1991). Psychiatric disorders in the parents of autistic individuals. *Journal of the American Academy of Child and Adolescent Psychiatry*, 30(3), 471−478. doi:10.1097/00004583-199105000-00019

Piven, J., Hurley, R., Losh, M., Parlier, M., & Reznick, J. S. (2008). Response to: Genichi Sugihara, Kenji J. Tsuchiya, Nori Takei, letter to the editor: Broad autism phenotype from schizophrenia-spectrum disorders. *Journal of Autism and Developmental Disorders*, 38(10), 2000−2001. doi:10.1007/s10803-008-0595-1

Piven, J., Palmer, P., Jacobi, D., Childress, D., & Arndt, S. (1997a). Broader autism phenotype: Evidence from a family history study of multiple-incidence autism families. *American Journal of Psychiatry*, 154(2), 185−190.

Piven, J., Palmer, P., Landa, R., Santangelo, S., Jacobi, D., & Childress, D. (1997b). Personality and language characteristics in parents from multiple-incidence autism families. *American Journal of Medical Genetics (Neuropsychiatric Genetics)*, 74(4), 398−411. doi:10.1002/(SICI)1096-8628(19970725)74:4 < 398::AID-AJMG11 > 3.0.CO;2-D

Piven, J., & Sasson, N. J. (2014). On the misapplication of the Broad Autism Phenotype Questionnaire in a study of autism. *Journal of Autism and Developmental Disorders*, 44(8), 2077−2078. doi:10.1007/s10803-014-2076-z

Piven, J., Vieland, V. J., Parlier, M., Thompson, A., O'Conner, I., Woodbury-Smith, M., ... Szatmari, P. (2013). A molecular genetic study of autism and related phenotypes in extended pedigrees. *Journal of Neurodevelopmental Disorders*, 5(30). (Open access article). Retrieved from http://www.jneurodevdisorders.com/content/5/1/30

Piven, J., Wrozek, M., Landa, R., Lainhart, J., Bolton, P., Chase, G. A., & Folstein, S. (1994). Personality characteristics of the parents of autistic individuals. *Psychological Medicine*, 24(3), 783−795. doi:10.1017/S0033291700027938

Poljac, E., Poljac, E., & Yeung, N. (2012). Cognitive control of intentions for voluntary actions in individuals with a high level of autistic traits. *Journal of Autism and Developmental Disorders, 42*(12), 2523–2533. doi:10.1007/s10803-012-1509-9

Posserud, M.-B., Lundervold, A. J., & Gillberg, C. (2009). Validation of the Autism Spectrum Screening Questionnaire in a total population sample. *Journal of Autism and Developmental Disorders, 39*(1), 126–134. doi:10.1007/s10803-008-0609-z

Robel, L., Rousselot-Pailley, B., Fortin, C., Levy-Rueff, M., Golse, B., & Falissard, B. (2014). Subthreshold traits of the broad autistic spectrum are distributed across different subgroups in parents, but not siblings, of probands with autism. *European Child and Adolescent Psychiatry, 23*(4), 225–233. doi:10.1007/s00787-013-0451-5

Robins, D. L. (2008). Screening for autism spectrum disorders in primary care settings. *Autism, 12*(5), 537–556. doi:10.1177/1362361308094502

Robins, D. L., Fein, D., Barton, M. L., & Green, J. A. (2001). The Modified Checklist for Autism in Toddlers: An initial study investigating the early detection of autism and pervasive developmental disorders. *Journal of Autism and Developmental Disorders, 31*(2), 131–144. doi:10.1023/A:1010738829569

Roth, I. (2010). *The autism spectrum in the 21st century: Exploring psychology, biology and practice*. Philadelphia, PA: Jessica Kingsley Publishers.

Ruta, L., Mazzone, D., Mazzone, L., Wheelwright, S., & Baron-Cohen, S. (2012). The Autism-Spectrum Quotient-Italian version: A cross-cultural confirmation of the broader autism phenotype. *Journal of Autism and Developmental Disorders, 42*(4), 625–633. doi:10.1007/s10803-011-1290-1

Rutter, M. (2013). Changing concepts and findings on autism. *Journal of Autism and Developmental Disorders, 43*(8), 1749–1757. doi:10.1007/s10803-012-1713-7

Rutter, M., & Folstein, S. (1995). *Family history interview for developmental disorders of cognition and social functioning*. Unpublished interview.

Santangelo, S. L., & Folstein, S. E. (1995). Social deficits in the families of autistic probands. *American Journal of Human Genetics, 57*(4 Suppl.), A20.

Sasson, N. J., Lam, K. S. L., Childress, D., Parlier, M., Daniels, J. L., & Piven, J. (2013a). The Broad Autism Phenotype Questionnaire: Prevalence and diagnostic classification. *Autism Research, 6*(2), 134–143. doi:10.1002/aur.1272

Sasson, N. J., Lam, K. S. L., Parlier, M., Daniels, J. L., & Piven, J. (2013b). Autism and the broad autism phenotype: Familial and intergenerational transmission. *Journal of Neurodevelopmental Disorders, 5*(1), 11. (Open access article). doi:10.1186/1866-1955-5-11

Scheeren, A. M., & Stauder, J. E. A. (2008). Broader autism phenotype in parents of autistic children: Reality or myth? *Journal of Autism and Developmental Disorders, 38*(2), 276–287. doi:10.1007/s10803-007-0389-x

Seidman, I., Yirmiya, N., Milshtein, S., Ebstein, R. P., & Levi, S. (2012). The Broad Autism Phenotype Questionnaire: Mothers versus fathers of children with an autism spectrum disorder. *Journal of Autism and Developmental Disorders, 42*(5), 837–846. doi:10.1007/s10803-011-1315-9

Skuse, D., Warrington, R., Bishop, D., Chowdhury, U., Lau, J., Mandy, W., & Place, M. (2004). The Developmental, Dimensional and Diagnostic Interview (3di): A novel computerized assessment for autism spectrum disorders. *Journal of the American Academy of Child and Adolescent Psychiatry, 43*(5), 548–558. doi:10.1097/00004583-200405000-00008

Smith, C. J., Lang, C. M., Kryzak, L., Reichenberg, A., Hollander, E., & Silverman, J. M. (2009). Familial associations of intense preoccupations, an empirical factor of the restricted, repetitive behaviors and interests domain of autism. *Journal of Child Psychology and Psychiatry, 50*(8), 982–990. doi:10.1111/j.1469-7610.2009.02060.x

Stewart, M. E., & Austin, E. J. (2009). The structure of the Autism-Spectrum Quotient: Evidence from a student sample in Scotland. *Personality and Individual Differences, 47*(3), 224–228. doi:10.1016/j.paid.2009.03.004

Sugihara, G., Tsuchiya, K. J., & Takei, N. (2008). Distinguishing broad autism phenotype from schizophrenia-spectrum disorders. (Letter to the editor). *Journal of Autism and Developmental Disorders, 38*(10), 1998–1999. doi:10.1007/s10803-008-0638-7

Sung, Y. J., Dawson, G., Munson, J., Estes, A., Schellenberg, G. D., & Wijsman, E. M. (2005). Genetic investigation of quantitative traits related to autism: Use of multivariate polygenic models with ascertainment adjustment. *American Journal of Human Genetics, 76*(1), 68–81. doi:10.1086/426951

Tyrer, P., & Alexander, J. (1979). Classification of personality disorder. *British Journal of Psychiatry, 135*(2), 163–167. doi:10.1192/bjp.135.2.163

Tyrer, P., Alexander, M. S., Cicchetti, D., Cohen, M. S., & Remington, M. (1979). Reliability of a schedule for rating personality disorders. *British Journal of Psychiatry, 135*(2), 168–174. doi:10.1192/bjp.135.2.168

Wainer, A. L., Ingersoll, B. R., & Hopwood, C. J. (2011). The structure and nature of the broader autism phenotype in a non-clinical sample. *Journal of Psychopathology and Behavioral Assessment, 13*(4), 459–469. doi:10.1007/s10862-011-9259-0

Wheelwright, S., Auyeung, B., Allison, C., & Baron-Cohen, S. (2010). Defining the broader, medium and narrow autism phenotype among parents using the Autism Spectrum Quotient (AQ). *Molecular Autism, 1,* 10. (Open access article). doi:10.1186/2040-2392-1-10

Whitehouse, A. J. O., & Bishop, D. V. M. (2009). *The Children's Communication Checklist – Adult version (CC-A).* London: Pearson.

Whitehouse, A. J. O., Coon, H., Miller, J., Salisbury, B., & Bishop, D. V. M. (2010). Narrowing the broader autism phenotype: A study using the Communication Checklist – Adult Version (CC-A). *Autism, 14*(6), 559–574. doi:10.1177/1362361310382107

CHAPTER 3

GENETIC ASPECTS OF THE BROAD AUTISM PHENOTYPE

When Leo Kanner first identified autism spectrum disorder (ASD) as a distinct category of developmental disability, he also observed some characteristics of ASD among family members of affected individuals. For example, Kanner noted that parents of children with ASD were drawn to the arts and sciences but often showed only minimal interest in other people. Similarities between children with ASD and their parents, such as a reduced level of social interest, were assumed to be of psychogenic origin. Through the mid-1970s, the prevailing view about the etiology of ASD was Bruno Bettelheim's psychodynamically oriented belief that ASD stemmed from cold, uninvolved parenting (Losh, Adolphs, & Piven, 2011).

The landmark study by Folstein and Rutter (1977) instead directed attention to genetic factors as important in the etiology of ASD. As discussed in Chapter 1, their study of twins with ASD found high rates of concordance among identical twins, thus strongly implicating genetics as causally relevant. Folstein and Rutter's study prompted interest in the genetics of the broad autism phenotype (BAP) as well (Losh et al., 2011).

Evidence for the involvement of genetics in the BAP comes from twin studies showing a BAP concordance rate of 60–90% for monozygotic twins versus only 5–10% concordance among dizygotic twins (Losh, Sullivan, Trembath, & Piven, 2008b; Marco & Skuse, 2006). In addition to twin studies, family studies also have been employed to investigate BAP genetics. More recently, scientists have utilized genotyping and other biological research techniques to identify specific BAP candidate genes. This chapter will summarize the findings of studies that elucidate the genetics of the BAP.

3.1. FAMILY STUDIES

Bolton et al. (1994) performed the first family study regarding BAP genetics. These investigators sought to obtain information about what they called a "lesser variant of autism" (p. 877) in the hope of learning about its boundaries and its mode of inheritance. They recruited family members of 99 autism probands and compared these participants with family members of 36 individuals with Down syndrome. Interview data from the first-degree relatives of index cases with either autism or Down syndrome revealed group differences, with family members of autism probands more likely to show deficits in communication and social functioning.

To examine the boundaries of the BAP, Bolton and colleagues (1994) excluded data obtained from parents and reran their analyses using data from siblings of index cases. Even after excluding siblings with ASD, the researchers still noticed that social and communication deficits, as well as stereotyped behaviors, were found significantly more often among siblings of autism probands. Bolton et al. discovered that depending on how they defined their so-called lesser variant of ASD, from 12.4% to 20.4% of autism siblings manifested features of the BAP. In comparison, the same could be said for only 1.6–3.2% of participants whose siblings had Down syndrome.

Bolton and associates (1994) pointed out that the existence of ASD-like traits in siblings of autism probands could not be due solely to the stress of having a sibling with a disability, because rates of the BAP in siblings were similar whether they were born before or after the index cases. The much lower rate of BAP symptoms among siblings of Down syndrome lent further support to their argument. This team of scientists concluded that the boundaries of the BAP extended beyond traditionally defined autism and most likely involved multiple genes (Bolton et al., 1994).

Ghaziuddin (1997) studied parents of three individuals who had been diagnosed with both autism and Down syndrome. He noted that these parents exhibited characteristics of the BAP such as introversion, social isolation, perfectionism, and a preference for routines. Ghaziuddin believed that the children's autism was most likely due to genetic transmission from their parents, because neither their deficits in communication and social functioning nor their repetitive behaviors could be explained on the basis of Down syndrome alone.

Conducting a somewhat larger follow-up study, Ghaziuddin (2000) included 8 more people with both autism and Down syndrome and their families, for a total of 11 such families. He also recruited a comparison group of seven youngsters with only Down syndrome and their families.

Among the children with both autism and Down syndrome, seven parents met criteria for the BAP while the same was true of only one parent in the comparison group. Ghaziuddin also looked at the siblings of each group. Four of 11 siblings of people with both Down syndrome and autism were classified with the BAP, whereas none of the siblings in the comparison group had the BAP. Ghaziuddin surmised that "... autism-specific genetic factors" (p. 562) were responsible for the presence of autism in children who also had been diagnosed with Down syndrome. These factors manifested as the BAP in first-degree relatives. However, Ghaziuddin also observed that in connection with four cases of Down syndrome plus autism in his study, no first-degree relatives were identified with the BAP. Therefore, he speculated that in addition to genetics, unknown environmental factors might be related to the causation of ASD.

Starr et al. (2001) performed a study to examine whether the BAP was found among families of individuals who had both autism and significant cognitive impairment. They identified 47 index cases of people with autism whose intelligence quotient (IQ) scores were below 50, and gathered data about the relatives of these probands using the Family History Interview from Bolton et al.'s (1994) investigation. Starr and colleagues found that nearly 16% of the index cases' first-degree relatives (i.e., parents and siblings) could be classified with the BAP, as well as almost 8% of their second-degree relatives (i.e., grandparents, half-siblings, uncles, aunts, cousins, nephews, and nieces). When comparing their data to the findings of Bolton et al. (1994), Starr et al. noticed that prevalence rates of the BAP among first- and second-degree relatives of index cases were quite similar across both studies. Thus, they determined that familial loading for the BAP is roughly the same whether or not the index cases have significant intellectual disability.

Lainhart et al. (2002) looked at the BAP in relation to regressive ASD. This form of ASD involves normal development for the first one to two years of a child's life, followed by a sudden loss of skills that is most noticeable concerning language ability. At the time of the study, it was not yet clear whether environmental events (e.g., the administration of vaccines) might be responsible for observable regression to ASD after seemingly typical development. Lainhart and her colleagues posited that if vaccines or other environmental factors triggered regression into ASD, then rates of the BAP among relatives of children with regressive ASD should be comparable to rates of the BAP in the general population.

Participants in Lainhart et al.'s (2002) investigation included 18 parents whose children had regressive ASD and 70 parents whose children had ASD without regression. They were evaluated for BAP status using the

Modified Personality Assessment Schedule-Revised (MPAS-R; Piven et al., 1997b), the Pragmatic Rating Scale (Landa et al., 1992), and the Friendship Interview (Santangelo & Folstein, 1995). According to results, rates of the BAP were comparable in both groups of parents: approximately 28% of parents of children with regressive ASD, and roughly 33% of parents of children with non-regressive ASD. Lainhart et al. then found published data about the rate of the BAP in the general populace, which was reported to be under 4%. When compared to the population at large, rates of the BAP in both groups of parents who participated in this study were significantly higher. Lainhart et al. interpreted their results as showing that genetic liability to ASD is comparable for both regressive and non-regressive forms of ASD. They further stated that environmental events did not seem likely as the sole causal factor for regressive ASD, although they did conjecture that such events might have an additive effect on people who already had a genetic predisposition toward ASD.

A more recent study by Losh et al. (2012) examined the BAP in relation to a disorder that is associated with cognitive impairment, namely Fragile X syndrome. Recognizing symptom similarities between Fragile X and ASD, Losh et al. wondered whether they might find BAP characteristics among pre-mutation carriers of the *FMR1* gene that underlies Fragile X syndrome. Participants in their research consisted of three groups: 49 pre-mutation carriers who were mothers of children with Fragile X syndrome, 89 mothers of children with ASD, and a control group of 23 mothers of neurotypical children. Losh et al. (2012) used the Modified Personality Assessment Schedule (Tyrer, 1988) to measure BAP personality traits, as well as the Pragmatic Language Scale (Landa et al., 1992) to assess BAP language characteristics. They learned that in comparison to the control group, participants in both of the other two groups were more likely to display personality and language features of the BAP. Specifically, these two groups were more likely to show the personality trait of rigidity and they made the same kinds of pragmatic language errors. Based on these findings, Losh and colleagues suggested that the *FMR1* gene may be involved in subtle aspects of the BAP.

Another recent study explored whether having two parents who fit the definition of the BAP is more common for children with ASD. Sasson, Lam, Parlier, Daniels, and Piven (2013) recruited 711 biological parents of children with ASD from an autism registry in North Carolina. They also located a comparison group of 981 community-dwelling parents whose children had not been screened for developmental disorders, nor had the parents themselves been screened for such conditions. Sasson and colleagues reasoned that BAP characteristics would be evident in their comparison group at the same rate that would be found in the general population. The researchers evaluated both groups of parents with the Broad Autism Phenotype Questionnaire (BAPQ; Hurley, Losh, Parlier, Reznick, & Piven, 2007). Parents completed the BAPQ self-report as well as an informant report about the other biological parent of their child. To lessen the possibility of biased responses due to participants' personal beliefs about ASD, the BAPQ was administered using the title "The Personality and Preferences Questionnaire."

Results of this investigation indicated that only 4.3% of parental pairs of a child with ASD consisted of parents who both had the BAP. In addition, just over 15% of the parental pairs were comprised of parents who both demonstrated at least one feature of the BAP. The percentage of parental couples who both had the BAP was higher among parents of children with ASD than among parents in the comparison group; nevertheless, this percentage was low. On the other hand, almost 1/3 of the parental pairs of children with ASD had just one parent who met criteria for the BAP. Also, about 40% of the parental pairs of ASD parents had only one parent who had at least one BAP trait. Therefore, Sasson et al. determined that in at least a third of families, parents transmitted ASD characteristics to their children in a manner that did not involve new mutations.

In the Sasson et al. (2013) investigation, the children with ASD were evaluated using the Social Communication Questionnaire (SCQ; Rutter, Bailey, & Lord, 2003). The authors of this study discovered that children who had at least one parent with BAP characteristics obtained higher SCQ scores, signifying more impaired ASD, than children whose parents did not have any BAP traits. Interestingly, however, children's SCQ scores did not differ based on whether two parents versus only one parent had BAP characteristics. Sasson and colleagues also found that the children of parents with an aloof personality tended to have higher SCQ scores than did children whose parents were not aloof. Additionally, children whose parents were both aloof and had pragmatic language deficits tended to score higher on the SCQ social subscale but not on the SCQ rigidity subscale. In other words, these children demonstrated greater impairment in social functioning. Therefore, Sasson and colleagues wrote that the presence of the BAP in parents is both qualitatively and quantitatively related to ASD in children. They further hypothesized that social aspects of ASD show "intergenerational consistency" (p. 6) and that "separable BAP features may relate differentially to genetic liability to autism" (p. 6). Their major conclusion was that among parents of children with ASD, it is often the case that only one of the parents has features of the BAP. The results of this investigation support the strong heritability of ASD and suggest that the study of families containing members with BAP traits may lead to the identification of ASD-related genes.

3.2. SIMPLEX VERSUS MULTIPLEX FAMILY STUDIES

Research into the genetics of ASD and the BAP often draws a distinction between so-called simplex and multiplex families. A simplex family contains only one person with ASD, with no other detectable cases of ASD among first- through third-degree relatives of the index case (Davidson et al., 2012). The literature also has referred to these families as single-incidence families (Losh, Childress, Lam, & Piven, 2008a). Multiplex or multiple-incidence families have two or more children with ASD in a nuclear family (Losh et al., 2008a; Piven, Palmer, Jacobi, Childress, & Arndt, 1997a).

Scientists differentiate these two types of families due to their assumptions about the genetic factors responsible for causing only one versus several family members to be affected by ASD. It is believed that ASD in a simplex family is the result of so-called de novo, or new, mutations involving "submicroscopic deletions and duplications" of genetic material (Fischbach & Lord, 2010, p. 192). Genetic regions that contain either deletions or duplications are known as copy number variations or CNVs. CNVs also may result from the insertion of genes into the wrong place within an individual's genome (Copy number variation, 2008). In a simplex family, a new and rarely occurring CNV presumably exerts a major effect that leads to the development of ASD in the diagnosed person (Sucksmith, Roth, & Hoekstra, 2011; Virkud, Todd, Abbacchi, Zhang, & Constantino, 2008). Therefore, one potential way to identify genes associated with ASD is by comparing the genes of affected people in simplex families to the genes of their unaffected relatives (Fischbach & Lord, 2010).

Different assumptions pertain to the genetic makeup of multiplex families. Members of multiple-incidence families may have a greater genetic vulnerability for ASD than individuals from simplex families (Losh et al., 2008a; Piven et al., 1997a). According to Sucksmith et al. (2011), "subthreshold autistic traits aggregate in multiple-incidence ('multiplex') families" (p. 389). Each of these subthreshold traits may occur commonly in the general population, and each of them exerts only minor influence on a behavioral phenotype by itself. However, several of these commonly occurring genetic features may be transmitted to offspring, in whom they presumably interact to produce

ASD (Virkud et al., 2008). Therefore, undiagnosed relatives of ASD probands in multiplex families may be more likely to display characteristics of the BAP (Bernier, Gerdts, Munson, Dawson, & Estes, 2012).

A data set that serves as a resource for the study of simplex families is the Simons Simplex Collection (SSC). The Simons Foundation Autism Research Initiative created the SSC for the purpose of finding de novo mutations that confer risk for ASD (Fischbach & Lord, 2010). Over 2,000 simplex families participated in this initiative, which used stringent phenotyping methods to determine which families qualified for inclusion in the data set (Davidson et al., 2012).

Davidson and associates (2012) accessed data from the SSC to examine rates of the BAP in 1,650 simplex families. When participating adults were evaluated for inclusion in the SSC, they routinely completed the following three assessments: the self-report version of the BAPQ (Hurley et al., 2007), the Social Responsiveness Scale: Adult Research Version (SRS: ARV; Constantino & Gruber, 2005), and the Family History Interview-Interviewer Impressions (FHI-II; International Molecular Genetic Study of Autism Consortium, 2000). Davidson et al. compared assessment data from mothers and fathers in the sample and noticed several gender differences. Females obtained significantly higher scores on the Cognition and Mannerisms scales of the SRS: ARV, signifying more impairment in these domains. Males scored significantly higher on three other SRS: ARV scales, namely the scales for Awareness, Communication, and Motivation. In addition, males scored higher than females on the BAPQ total score and on all three domains of the BAPQ, that is, Aloofness, Rigidity, and Pragmatic Language. Most importantly, Davidson and colleagues (2012) learned that the majority of parents in their study could not be categorized as having the BAP according to any of the three assessment instruments. Therefore, they concluded that among simplex families, only a low rate of the BAP can be found. This research team further recognized that reliable measures of BAP characteristics are needed so that they can be used to identify connections between BAP features and particular CNVs.

Several studies have looked at the BAP in multiplex families. According to Piven (1999), such families "offer an important, high risk group for genetic studies of the BAP" (p. 301). An early investigation of this population by Piven et al. (1997a) sought to determine the prevalence of the BAP in parents of families containing at least two children with ASD. The researchers located 25 mothers and 23 fathers from 25 multiplex ASD families, which they compared to a group of 30 mothers and 30 fathers from 30 families of a child with Down syndrome. All of these parents completed the FHI (Bolton et al., 1994) to determine their BAP status. During the interview they also were questioned about the siblings, grandparents, first cousins, aunts, and uncles of the ASD index cases. Piven and colleagues reported that in comparison to Down syndrome parents, the ASD parents revealed significantly higher rates of repetitive behaviors and deficits in social functioning. In particular, 20% of the mothers of children with ASD demonstrated communication deficits, while none of the mothers of children with Down syndrome showed these deficiencies. Similar findings were obtained when comparing the grandparents, aunts, and uncles of ASD probands to the same kinds of relatives of children with Down syndrome. Furthermore, social impairment was evident in ASD siblings whereas the siblings of children with Down syndrome did not exhibit such problems. Due to the elevated rates of stereotyped behaviors, communication deficits, and difficulties in social functioning that were identified in multiplex ASD family members, Piven et al. urged other researchers to include individuals with the BAP in studies exploring the genetics of ASD.

Focusing on siblings of children with ASD, Constantino, Zhang, Frazier, Abbacchi, and Law (2010) recruited a large sample of 1,235 families to examine the genetics of ASD. They divided their sample into three subgroups: (1) multiple-incidence families; (2) single-incidence families containing a child with ASD, but in which no other children showed either ASD or language delays; and (3) single-incidence families in which at least one additional child without ASD had a history of language delays and autism-like speech. Among the findings that related to the BAP, Constantino et al. noted that 20% of non-diagnosed siblings in this study had experienced language delays and one-half of these demonstrated autism-like speech characteristics. In addition, non-diagnosed male siblings in multiplex families were more likely than non-diagnosed siblings in simplex families to display ASD traits as indicated by scores on a quantitative measure of ASD traits, the SRS (Constantino & Gruber, 2005). According to Constantino et al., the results of their investigation supported the idea that different modes of genetic transmission apply in simplex families versus multiplex families. They further recommended that siblings and other first-degree relatives of ASD probands should be included as participants in future research, because doing so may allow for the identification of genes associated with diagnosable ASD and related subclinical syndromes.

Two studies explored the BAP in parents of multiplex families. Losh et al. (2008a) compared parents from simplex and multiplex families regarding their language, social, and personality characteristics. This scientific team speculated that they would find a continuum of ASD traits, with

the strongest expression of these traits observable among multiplex parents. Somewhat lesser expression of such traits was expected among simplex parents, and parents of children with Down syndrome were believed to be least likely of the three parent groups to demonstrate ASD features. Participants in the Losh et al. (2008a) investigation included parents from 25 multiplex ASD families, parents from 35 simplex ASD families, and parents of 30 children with Down syndrome. They were assessed for the presence of BAP characteristics using questionnaires that examined their personality features, social behavior, and pragmatic language abilities. An exploratory factor analysis of these data yielded four factors that reflected features of the BAP: language difficulties, rigid personality, anxiety, and social deficits. Next, participants were evaluated according to whether they displayed none, one, or several of these four features. Results supported the hypotheses made by Losh et al. at the onset of their research. In most of the multiple-incidence ASD families, both parents exhibited BAP traits. Simplex families, however, were just as likely to contain two parents, one parent, or no parents with BAP characteristics. In fact, neither parent displayed any BAP features in half of the simplex families. Therefore, Losh and colleagues surmised that multiple-incidence ASD families contain greater genetic loading for ASD. They suggested that each parent in a multiplex family has a genetic makeup that by itself is expressed as the BAP; however, the genes of parents from multiplex families combine and interact in a manner that leads to ASD in their children. On the basis of these suppositions, Losh and associates further inferred that the genetic composition of the BAP must be less complex than the genetic makeup of ASD.

Bernier et al. (2012) also conducted an exploration of simplex versus multiplex ASD families, using not one by two comparison groups. In addition to 39 parents from multiple-incidence ASD families and 22 parents from single-incidence ASD families, participants in this study included 20 parents of children with developmental delays other than ASD, as well as 20 parents of neurotypical children. All four groups of parents were interviewed using the Broader Phenotype Autism Symptom Scale (BPASS; Dawson et al., 2007). This instrument measures four domains of the BAP: social interest, nonverbal social communication, conversational ability, and the interviewee's range and intensity of interests. Multivariate statistical analyses revealed that parents from multiplex families displayed significantly more BAP features than parents in any of the other groups. Another notable finding was that parents from simplex families did not differ from the two non-ASD groups. The researchers determined that social and communication features of the BAP are more likely to be present in parents from multiplex ASD families than in simplex ASD parents. Bernier and colleagues also cited their results as supportive of the notion that mechanisms of genetic transmission in multiple-incidence ASD families differ from those of single-incidence ASD families.

3.3. TWIN STUDIES

The twin study is another research method that has been used to examine the genetics of the BAP. This approach capitalizes on what is known about the genetic makeup of identical (monozygotic) versus fraternal (dizygotic) twins. Because monozygotic twins arise from the same fertilized ovum, they have the same genetic endowment. However, dizygotic twins arise from two separate sperm−ovum combinations and therefore are only as genetically similar as any other pair of siblings. In other words, fraternal twins have only 50% of their genes in common. Therefore, when a higher degree of similarity for a given trait is evident among identical twins in comparison to fraternal twins, genetic factors are presumed to be responsible for the trait (Whitbourne & Halgin, 2014).

The main purpose of a twin study by Bailey et al. (1995) was to examine the genetics of narrowly defined autism. (This investigation is described in greater detail in Chapter 1.) However, when this research team employed a broader definition of autism, they discovered that 92% of identical twin pairs were concordant for social and cognitive impairments as compared to only 10% of fraternal twins. Thus, Bailey and colleagues reported that genetic features seem to be involved in the etiology of the BAP.

Le Couteur et al. (1996) explored the genetics of the BAP in a sample of 28 monozygotic and 20 same-sex dizygotic twin pairs, among which at least one twin in each pair met criteria for autism. (This study is described more fully in Chapter 1.) These investigators created an operational definition of the BAP that focused on communication and social deficits such as delayed speech and reading in childhood, limited friendships, conversational difficulties, and unusual behavior. Nine of the identical twin pairs in their study were discordant for traditionally defined autism, but seven of these monozygotic pairs contained an individual who was classified as having the BAP. In contrast, the BAP was found in only 2 of the 20 fraternal twin pairs. The statistical difference between the two groups was highly significant, supporting the premise that genetic factors are strongly related to the BAP. Yet another pertinent result of the study by Le Couteur and associates was that repetitive behaviors were observed in only one-third of the twins who had the BAP. Freitag (2007) interpreted this finding as an indication that the genetic factors leading to stereotyped behavior are different from those that underlie social and communication impairments.

Beyond looking only at twin pairs in which one twin has been diagnosed with ASD, some twin studies have looked at ASD traits in the general population. For example, Constantino and Todd (2003) obtained a randomly selected sample of 788 twin pairs from an epidemiologic investigation known as the Missouri Twin Study. Parents were asked to complete the SRS (Constantino, 2002) for each of their offspring in a twin pair; this questionnaire yields a quantitative measure of ASD traits. Based on the analyses of their data, the authors of this study determined that autistic traits are continuously distributed throughout a general populace. They further described these traits as "moderately to highly heritable" (Constantino & Todd, 2003, p. 524), and noted that the cutoff between ASD and unaffected individuals is arbitrary.

More recently, an investigation by Hoekstra, Bartels, Verweij, and Boomsma (2007) looked for ASD traits among a general population of twins in the Netherlands, as well as their parents and siblings. These scientists also wished to learn whether assortative mating might contribute to the higher prevalence rates of ASD traits that are commonly noticed in first-degree relatives of ASD index cases. The term *assortative mating* refers to "nonrandom partner choice" (Hoekstra et al., 2007, p. 373). With regard to the BAP and ASD, assortative mating describes the supposition that individuals with ASD traits might seek partners who tend toward introversion and prefer behavioral routines (Hoekstra et al., 2007).

The Netherlands Twin Register enabled Hoekstra and colleagues (2007) to recruit 194 families of twins. This sample included 370 adult twins, 94 siblings, and 128 couples who were parents of twins. Participants completed the Dutch version of the Autism-Spectrum Quotient (AQ; Baron-Cohen, Wheelwright, Skinner, Martin, & Clubley, 2001b), an instrument that provides a quantitative measure of autistic traits. Similar to outcomes reported by Constantino and Todd (2003), results of this study revealed that "autistic traits are continuously distributed in the population" (Hoekstra et al., 2007, p. 372). Model-fitting analyses indicated that genetic influences in individual differences for ASD traits are important, accounting for 57% of the variance in this study's data. Correlations between identical twins were higher than between fraternal twins, again implying that genetics play a role in these characteristics. However, because correlations between identical twins were not twice as high as for fraternal twins, Hoekstra and associates stated that shared environment also might be relevant. These researchers found no evidence of assortative mating and concluded that "in the general population, there is no passive or active partner selection for autistic traits" (p. 372).

When considering the latter two twin studies mentioned above, two common findings emerge. First, ASD traits are continuously distributed in a general population. Second, both studies report that genetics play a role in the causation of these features. These findings pertain to the BAP because individuals who meet criteria for the BAP are included in a general population and harbor subclinical, heritable features of ASD.

3.4. ENDOPHENOTYPES

The study of BAP genetics sometimes involves the identification of endophenotypes, which are "inherited, quantitative phenotypic components of a syndrome" (Constantino, 2011b, p. 516). Endophenotypes may be physiological, behavioral, or neuropsychological, and are evident in both affected and unaffected individuals (Constantino, 2011a; Losh et al., 2008b). In fact, they are typically more prevalent in unaffected relatives than in a general population (Alarcon, Yonan, Gilliam, Cantor, & Geschwind, 2005; Saresella et al., 2009). Researchers who study ASD are interested in endophenotypes not only to better understand the BAP, but to locate specific genetic influences on the etiology of ASD (Cantor, 2011; Losh et al., 2008b).

In an early search to identify such genetic components, Sung et al. (2005) obtained a sample of 201 families containing 694 members. These were multiplex nuclear families, each of which contained at least two children with ASD or some of its symptoms. Among the 201 families, 15 contained members who were classified as having the BAP. These individuals did not meet criteria for a diagnosable ASD but did exhibit communicative deficits, social impairment, and/or repetitive behaviors. Sung and colleagues administered a preliminary, unpublished version of the BPASS (Dawson et al., 2007) to measure ASD features of their participants. This instrument assesses the traits of nonverbal expressiveness, conversational ability, age of language acquisition, degree of social motivation, and flexibility and range of interests. Furthermore, it provides a quantification of ASD traits and can be used "among all family members, both children and adults, with and without ASD" (Sung et al., 2005, p. 71). When BPASS data were subjected to multivariate analyses, Sung et al. discerned that the traits of social motivation and flexibility/range of interests demonstrated the highest heritability and were most strongly correlated. They reported that these two features might be genetically related and thus might warrant further study using gene mapping. Extrapolating from the work of Sung et al., it appears that the BPASS domains of social motivation and flexibility/range of interests might serve as endophenotypes for the BAP and ASD.

Alarcon et al. (2005) chose to focus instead on aspects of language and repetitive behavior, using items from the Autism Diagnostic Interview-Revised (ADI-R; Lord, Rutter, & Le Couteur, 1994) as ASD endophenotypes. One of these measured the age when participants spoke their first word, and another assessed the age at which they spoke their first phrase. A third endophenotype combined three ADI-R items to create a composite measure of repetitive behavior. Participants in the Alarcon et al. investigation consisted of 291 multiple-incidence autism families from the Autism Genetic Resource Exchange (AGRE). Each of these nuclear families included at least two children with possible ASD. Although some participants had narrowly defined autism, others did not meet full criteria but did show some ASD features. According to the authors, some of the participants displayed only minimal deficits. Therefore, participants in this study varied in position along the autism continuum, with some having marked impairment and others having only mild problems. Due to their membership in the AGRE database, the members of this sample had already undergone genotyping.

Employing a technique called ordered-subsets analysis, Alarcon and colleagues (2005) identified quantitative trait loci related to their chosen endophenotypes. A *quantitative trait locus* (QTL) is a portion of a chromosome that contains genes for a specific trait (Cantor, 2011). The researchers found connections between age at first word and QTLs on the long arms of chromosomes 3, 7, and 17. They also identified a relationship between age at first spoken phrase and a QTL on chromosome 17.

In 2007, Losh and Piven chose performance on the revised version of the Eyes Test (Baron-Cohen, Wheelwright, Hill, Raste, & Plumb, 2001a) as an endophenotype for the BAP. This test of social cognition measures the ability to identify complex mental states and feelings based on viewing pictures that show only the eye area of a face. Participants in the Losh and Piven (2007) study included 48 parents of individuals with autism and 22 control parents. Both groups of parents were of similar average age and all of them had adequate intellectual functioning. In addition to the Eyes Test, parents of children with autism were evaluated for the possible presence of the BAP using the MPAS-R (Piven et al., 1997b), the Friendship Interview (Piven et al., 1997b), and the Pragmatic Rating Scale (Landa et al., 1992). (These instruments are discussed in Chapter 2 in more detail.) Among these 48 parents, 13 were classified as aloof, 11 were categorized as rigid, and 24 of them did not show any features of the BAP. Statistical analyses indicated that the aloof parents performed significantly worse on the Eyes Test in comparison to control parents, as well as in comparison to non-aloof parents of children with autism. Interestingly, rigid parents' scores on the Eyes Test were comparable to those of control parents. Losh and Piven further noted that the impaired social cognition of aloof parents was linked to difficulties with pragmatic language and low-quality friendships. From these results, they concluded that impaired social cognition as measured by the Eyes Test was associated with other BAP characteristics, and they suggested the Eyes Test as an endophenotype that could be used in future genetic studies of the BAP and ASD.

Also in 2007, Duvall and colleagues used yet another instrument as an ASD endophenotype. This research team opted for the SRS (Constantino, 2002), discussed earlier in this chapter, as their measure of social functioning in multiplex autism families. Duvall et al. obtained a sample from the AGRE that included 190 index cases with autism and 57 unaffected siblings. Genotype information and SRS scores were available for these participants. Although the SRS scores of affected individuals differed significantly from those of unaffected siblings, the score distributions for these two groups overlapped quite a bit, indicating that SRS scores offer a quantitative measure of social relatedness. Linkage analyses using SRS scores pointed to a segment of chromosome 11 and a segment of chromosome 17 as genetic regions associated with social impairment. When these authors analyzed their data again using only male participants, they found that regions of chromosomes 4, 8, and 10 were identified in addition to the already-mentioned areas on chromosomes 11 and 17. Duvall et al. cited their results as evidence that the SRS is a useful endophenotype. However, they also highlighted the value of including seemingly unaffected siblings in such studies. As noted by this research team, siblings who are unaffected may be just below arbitrary cutoffs for a classification of ASD but still share genetic risk factors with their affected brothers or sisters.

An inquiry conducted by a research group in Italy examined differences in immune system functioning as a potential endophenotype for ASD. Based on the scientific literature, Saresella et al. (2009) knew that a variety of impairments in immune functioning (e.g., reductions in the total number of lymphocytes and defects in T cell activation, among others) already had been associated with ASD. Therefore, they hypothesized that similar dysfunctions might exist in unaffected siblings of children with ASD. Participants in their study included 20 children and adolescents with ASD, 15 siblings in a similar age range, and 20 neurotypical children and teens as controls. Blood samples were taken from these youngsters and analyzed for several types of immune dysfunction.

Upon reviewing their results, Saresella and colleagues (2009) observed that the immune functioning of siblings was significantly more similar to the immune functioning of the ASD group when compared with the group of typically developing youths. Both the ASD and sibling groups produced greater amounts of interleukin-10, which has powerful anti-inflammatory features. These two groups also demonstrated increased production of T lymphocytes but diminished numbers of $CD4^+$ and $CD8^+$ lymphocytes. Saresella and associates (2009) proposed that immunologic function could be used as a new kind of endophenotype for ASD.

Rapid automatized naming (RAN) was the proposed endophenotype in a 2010 investigation by Losh, Esserman, and Piven. This group of researchers selected RAN as an endophenotype on the basis of prior studies showing that parents of children with ASD were slower when performing RAN tasks such as naming colors or common objects. Previous research also had indicated that RAN ability was both quantitative and heritable (Losh, Esserman, & Piven, 2010).

Adults with high-functioning autism, their parents, and a control group of parents were administered parts of the RAN test (Denckla & Rudel, 1976), which required them to quickly name either primary colors or everyday objects presented in several rows. Participants also were assessed for the possible presence of the BAP using the MPAS-R (Piven et al., 1997b). According to evaluations from two independent raters, 86 participants exhibited social impairment consistent with the BAP, and 74 participants manifested the BAP feature of rigidity/perfectionism. Parents also were interviewed to check for a history of language delays, which yielded 70 participants who acknowledged such a history. Results demonstrated that in comparison to controls, both individuals with high-functioning autism and their parents needed significantly more time to complete the RAN test. Additionally, both the BAP social trait of aloofness and a history of delayed language were each associated with longer times to finish the RAN task. Losh et al. (2010) concluded that the RAN test could be helpful in molecular studies of ASD genetics, because RAN performance was linked to characteristics of the BAP and was apparent in both diagnosed and undiagnosed individuals in families containing members with ASD.

While both simplex and multiplex families participated in the Losh et al. (2010) investigation, members of only multiple-incidence families served as participants in an endophenotype study conducted by Nyden, Hagberg, Gousse, and Rastam (2011). This scientific team examined a "neurocognitive endophenotype of autism" (Nyden et al., 2011, p. 191), which they defined as including the psychological constructs of central coherence, executive functions, and theory of mind. According to these authors, the term *weak central coherence* denoted a tendency toward focusing on details rather than a situation as a whole; as a result, weak central coherence also adversely affects social ability. For purposes of this study, *executive functions* referred to capacities for planning ahead and for shifting attention. *Theory of mind* describes the ability to infer another person's mental state. Nyden and associates (2011) cited past research showing that deficits in all of these abilities are heritable and are more commonly found in family members of ASD index cases than in the general public.

Eighty-six individuals from 18 multiplex autism families took part in the Nyden et al. (2011) inquiry regarding a cognitive endophenotype. They completed a battery of neuropsychological tests including the Embedded Figures Test (EFT; Witkin, Oltman, Raskin, & Karp, 1971) to examine central coherence, the Tower of London test (Shallice, 1982) to assess planning ability, parts A and B of the Trail Making Test (Reitan, 1958) to measure the ability to shift attention, and a cartoon explanation task (Gallagher et al., 2000) to probe theory of mind ability. As shown by results of this study, the BAP does not appear to include weak central coherence, theory of mind deficits, or problems with attention-shifting among its characteristics. However, all members of these ASD families (i.e., fathers, mothers, children with autism, and their unaffected siblings) had trouble in the area of planning ability, as measured by the Tower of London task. Nyden and colleagues interpreted this finding as suggesting that visual scanning deficits may be a component of the ASD phenotype.

A team of scientists in the United Kingdom also examined two cognitive endophenotypes of ASD and the BAP. Spencer and associates (2011) opted to study siblings of people with ASD because siblings have a much higher risk for ASD than what is found in the general population. The researchers were interested in siblings' responses to social stimuli in the form of facial expressions. Because prior studies had amply documented that people with ASD display unusual responses to facial expressions, Spencer and colleagues wondered whether the same might hold true for the BAP. They recruited three groups of participants: 40 adolescents with ASD, 40 teens who were full biological siblings of the first group members, and a control group of 40 typically developing teenagers. Siblings and control participants were screened for possible ASD using the SCQ (Berument, Rutter, Lord, Pickles, & Bailey, 1999). All of them scored below the threshold on this measure, indicating that they did not appear to have ASD. The mean IQ score of the ASD group was significantly lower than the mean IQ for the other two groups; the ASD group functioned within the average range of intelligence while the other two groups had mean IQ scores in the high average range. However, there were no significant differences in IQ between the sibling and control groups.

During the Spencer et al. (2011) investigation, participants in all three groups were shown a series of 24 faces: 8 happy faces, 8 frightened faces, and 8 neutral faces. These were obtained from a commonly used standard array of facial expressions (Ekman & Friesen, 1975) and were interspersed with a series of eight crosses as visual fixation points. Participants underwent functional magnetic resonance imaging (fMRI) while viewing the visual stimuli. Scans from this procedure allowed the research team to observe patterns of brain activation in response to the various visual images that had been presented.

Eleven different brain regions were examined, and results indicated that siblings manifested brain activation between that of the ASD group and the control group. In comparison to the control group, siblings showed significantly reduced brain activation in the following seven brain regions: left superior frontal gyrus, right and left temporal poles, right middle and left posterior of the superior temporal sulcus, left dorsomedial prefrontal cortex, and right fusiform face area (Spencer et al., 2011). However, these responses were comparable to those from the ASD group. Furthermore, the researchers discerned that the observable differences between siblings' and controls' responses could be accounted for in terms of responses specifically to happy faces. Therefore, Spencer et al. (2011) concluded that fMRI responses to facial expressions could be useful as an ASD endophenotype.

In their second study (i.e., Spencer et al., 2012), this team of investigators noted that previous research has shown persons with ASD to demonstrate better-than-average performance on the EFT (Witkin et al., 1971). This task involves finding a target shape within a more complicated visual pattern. Similar to the study just described, Spencer and colleagues (2012) located 38 teens with ASD who had full biological siblings also in adolescence. Forty siblings also were recruited, as well as a control group of

40 neurotypical teens. Each of these three groups completed the AQ. As expected, the ASD group scored significantly higher on the AQ than the other two groups. Importantly, the mean AQ score for the sibling group was comparable to the control group mean.

Next, each of the participants completed the EFT while undergoing fMRI. This technology provided a series of 32 brain images for each participant, which enabled the researchers to determine patterns of brain activation during the process of taking the test. Spencer and associates (2012) learned that in comparison to the control group, both the ASD and sibling groups showed significantly more activation in the brain regions of the left anterior middle temporal gyrus, inferior frontal gyrus, and anterior superior temporal sulcus. Consequently, the authors suggested that an atypical pattern of fMRI activation when performing the EFT is "evidence for an atypical neural substrate of information processing during this task in autism and in the broader phenotype in siblings" (p. 3478). They further suggested that this unusual fMRI pattern could serve as an endophenotype in genetic studies.

Yet another cognitive endophenotype was suggested in a study by Fiorentini, Gray, Rhodes, Jeffery, and Pellicano (2012). Because relatives of people with ASD previously had been shown to process faces in an atypical fashion, these researchers chose to explore whether differences would manifest in a test of "face identity aftereffects" (Fiorentini et al., 2012, p. 2926). The test involves exposing participants to a target face. Once the target face is familiar, identity aftereffects create a bias to see a face shown later as having properties opposite to the original face. For example, if the target face has smaller than average lips, the aftereffect would lead to seeing a face with larger than average lips (Fiorentini et al., 2012). In this study, 20 parents and 8 siblings of children with ASD served as the experimental group, while 20 parents and 10 siblings of neurotypical children comprised the control group. The research protocol was presented to them in the form of a forced-choice game on a computer, involving police teams and robbers. During the first training phase of this study, the participants were introduced to grayscale photographs of two male faces and were told to look at the faces of these two "police team captains" for as long as they needed, until they could distinguish between the two men. In a second training phase, they were shown faces that were partially similar to the original two and were asked to tell whether these altered versions belonged with one or the other of the original faces. When presented with the adaptation phase of the study, participants were shown "antifaces" who were "robbers," followed by target faces of the "police" who caught them.

Participants were to name which police team caught the robber. According to their results, Fiorentini and colleagues discovered that in comparison to relatives of neurotypical children, the parents and siblings of children with ASD showed lesser aftereffects. The researchers construed this finding as evidence that facial coding of ASD relatives is less efficient, and nominated their research paradigm as an ASD endophenotype (Fiorentini et al., 2012).

3.5. MOLECULAR GENETIC STUDIES

Eapen (2011) described the BAP as the outcome of one or more genes that are commonly found throughout the general population, leading to a variety of phenotypes due to either gene–gene or gene–environment interactions. The possibility exists that individuals with the BAP may be endowed with fewer deleterious genes than would be found in individuals who have diagnosable ASD (Newshaffer et al., 2007). Support for this notion comes from the finding that some relatives of people with ASD display ASD-like features in only a single domain (Steyaert & De La Marche, 2008; Williams & Bowler, 2014), such as pragmatic language or social functioning. Due to the number of genes that might be involved, the complex mechanisms that govern how they are expressed, and the heterogeneity of the BAP's symptom presentation, it has been difficult for researchers to identify specific genes that confer susceptibility to ASD (Newshaffer et al., 2007; Spence, 2004).

A few studies of genome-wide scans of ASD genotypes have included examination of the BAP (Losh et al., 2008b). These studies have implicated regions of chromosomes 3, 7, 11, and 17 in connection with the BAP (Losh et al., 2008b). Linkage analyses also have suggested chromosome region 10p12-q11.1 and chromosome region 17p11.2-q12 as relevant to the BAP (Freitag, 2007). In addition, a segment of the X chromosome (specifically Xq27-q28) appears to be associated with the BAP (Vincent et al., 2005).

Some studies have been able to identify specific candidate genes for the BAP. For example, St. Pourcain and colleagues (2010) examined a gene called rs4307059 in a sample of 7,313 children who were involved in a longitudinal study of ASD in the United Kingdom. Genotype information was available for these children, who also were evaluated regarding 29 different measures of functioning which included measures of language and communication, intellectual ability, social functioning, behavioral problems, and special educational needs. Regression analyses indicated that an increased loading for the rs4307059 gene was linked to poorer conversational skills. St. Pourcain et al. proposed that this gene, which is a variant found on chromosome region 5p14.1, could serve as a QTL for the BAP in the general population.

An oxytocin receptor gene on chromosome 3 was the focus of an inquiry by Chen and Johnson (2012). They chose to investigate oxytocin because this hormone facilitates the forming and maintaining of social bonds, which involve abilities that may be deficient among people with the BAP. These researchers predicted that two variants of the *OXTR* gene, specifically rs2254298 and rs53576, would be associated with the BAP in the general populace, and that this relationship would be more commonly found among males. An ethnically diverse sample of 70 men and 108 women participated in the Chen and Johnson study. Participants completed the AQ (Baron-Cohen et al., 2001b) and gave saliva samples for genotyping. Results indicated that males scored significantly higher than females on the AQ; higher AQ scores signify a greater number of autism-like features. Also, males with at least one copy of a certain allele for *OXTR* rs2254298 (specifically the A allele) scored higher on the AQ than males with two copies of the alternate (G) allele. Therefore, Chen and Johnson reported, "This represents the first evidence of a significant relationship between oxytocin receptor gene polymorphisms and the BAP in males" (p. 97).

Jensen (2013) identified five other BAP candidate genes: *SLC6A4*, *COMT*, *MET*, *CNTNAP2*, and *FOXP2*. These and other BAP candidate genes are pleiotropic (Jensen, 2013), meaning that they are expressed in more than one phenotype (Geschwind, 2011). The five listed candidate genes are quite commonly found throughout the general population. *SLC6A4*, a serotonin transporter gene located in chromosome region 17q11-12, was one of the first genes proposed as an ASD candidate gene. Studies have linked this gene with depression, obsessive compulsive disorder (OCD), and rigid compulsions. *COMT*, found in chromosome region 22q11, has been associated with not only ASD but also anxiety, depression, OCD, and schizotypy. Chromosome region 7q31 is the home of the *MET* gene, which reportedly is associated with ASD as well as bipolar disorder, OCD, tics, and Tourette's syndrome. Both *CNTNAP2* and *FOXP2* are located in chromosome region 7q35. Research has connected them with developmental language disorder, OCD, dyslexia, selective mutism, and social anxiety (Jensen, 2013).

Finally, Piven and colleagues (2013) found still other BAP candidate genes by conducting linkage analyses among 19 "extended pedigrees" (p. 30), meaning that three or more cases of ASD existed across at least two nuclear families. Members of these families who did not have ASD were evaluated for the BAP using the MPAS-R (Piven et al., 1997b) and the Modified Pragmatic Rating Scale (Piven et al., 1997b). The latter instrument is a briefer version of an assessment device that identifies errors in grammar, prosody, and pragmatic language use. Also in this study, 322 individuals were genotyped, averaging 17 people per pedigree.

Piven and colleagues' (2013) linkage analyses for ASD and the BAP showed that the BAP gene loci generally correlated with ASD loci, indicating that "equating non-ASD relatives with non-carriers of ASD genes is not correct in general" (p. 41). However, considerable genetic variation was apparent among these families, with very few genetic loci found in common across them. Also of interest was the uncovering of some previously unidentified BAP loci. These novel loci occurred at chromosome regions 2q37.3, 11q23.3, 14q11.2, 14q31.3, and 15q13.3. Of these, only 2q37.2 also was significantly associated with ASD. Three other BAP loci (11q23.3, 14q11.2, and 14q31.3) were significant only for the BAP. Another noteworthy result was the discovery that the genetic region linked with repetitive behavior "appears to be entirely genetically independent of BAP" (Piven et al., 2013, p. 41). Due to the complexity of the genetics that underlie ASD and the BAP, the authors of this research suggested that future studies might benefit by using more and larger pedigrees that include the measurement of multiple characteristics, some of which should be biological (Piven et al., 2013).

Piven (2002) suggested that studies of the BAP could be useful for increasing knowledge about the genetics of personality. However, a more pressing reason for exploring the genetic makeup of the BAP is to identify genes that confer susceptibility to ASD. BAP genes are believed to give rise to ASD by interacting with "other gene mutations inherited and/or *de novo*, environmental risk factors and epigenetic events acting alone or in concert" (Jensen, 2013, p. 11). Environmental risk factors that are suspected of contributing to ASD include vitamin D deficiency during pregnancy or early childhood (Kocovska, Fernell, Billstedt, Minnis, & Gillberg, 2012), exposure to metals, flame retardants, bacterial and viral infections (Hertz-Picciotto et al., 2006), air pollution (Volk, Hertz-Picciotto, Delwiche, Lurmann, & McConnell, 2011), and pesticides (Hertz-Picciotto et al., 2006; Shelton, Hertz-Picciotto, & Pessah, 2012). The term *epigenetic* refers to processes that do not alter a DNA sequence but instead modify the way that DNA is transcribed, thus leading to a change of the way that the gene is expressed (Geschwind, 2011).

Because BAP genes are so widely distributed among the population at large, the identification of environmental risk factors that might be present during prenatal and neonatal development is crucial. Knowledge of such risk factors would increase the possibility of directing efforts toward the prevention of ASD (Jensen, 2013). Also, the inclusion of family members with the BAP in future molecular genetic studies will enhance the ability of such research to pinpoint candidate genes that comprise the BAP and contribute to the etiology of ASD (Buxbaum et al., 2001; Losh et al., 2011).

REFERENCES

Alarcon, M., Yonan, A. L., Gilliam, T. C., Cantor, R. M., & Geschwind, D. H. (2005). Quantitative genome scan and ordered-subsets analysis of autism endophenotypes support language QTLs. *Molecular Psychiatry, 10*(8), 747–757. doi:10.10138/sj.mp.4001666

Bailey, A., Le Couteur, A., Gottesman, I., Bolton, P., Simonoff, E., Yuzda, E., & Rutter, M. (1995). Autism as a strongly genetic disorder: Evidence from a British twin study. *Psychological Medicine, 25*(1), 63–77. doi:10.1017/S0033291700028099

Baron-Cohen, S., Wheelwright, S., Hill, J., Raste, Y., & Plumb, I. (2001). The 'reading the mind in the eyes' test revised version: A study with normal adults, and adults with Asperger syndrome or high-functioning autism. *Journal of Child Psychology and Psychiatry, 42*(2), 241–251. doi:10.1111/1469-7610.00715

Baron-Cohen, S., Wheelwright, S., Skinner, R., Martin, C. E., & Clubley, E. (2001). The Autism-spectrum Quotient (AQ): Evidence from Asperger syndrome/high-functioning autism, males and females, scientists and mathematicians. *Journal of Autism and Developmental Disorders, 31*(1), 5–17. doi:10.1023/A:1005653411471

Bernier, R., Gerdts, J., Munson, J., Dawson, G., & Estes, A. (2012). Evidence for broader autism phenotype characteristics in parents from multiple-incidence autism families. *Autism Research, 5*(1), 13–20. doi:10.1002/aur.226

Berument, S. K., Rutter, M., Lord, C., Pickles, A., & Bailey, A. (1999). Autism screening questionnaire: Diagnostic validity. *British Journal of Psychiatry, 175*(5), 444–451. doi:10.1192/bjp.175.5.444

Bolton, P., Macdonald, H., Pickles, A., Rios, P., Goode, S., Crowson, M., ... Rutter, M. (1994). A case-control family history study of autism. *Journal of Child Psychology and Psychiatry, 35*(5), 877–900. doi:10.1111/j.1469-7610.1994.tb02300.x

Buxbaum, J. D., Silverman, J. M., Smith, C. J., Kilifarski, M., Reichert, J., Hollander, E., ... Davis, K. L. (2001). Evidence for a susceptibility gene for autism on chromosome 2 and for genetic heterogeneity. *American Journal of Human Genetics, 68*(6), 1514–1520.

Cantor, R. M. (2011). Autism endophenotypes and quantitative trait loci. In D. G. Amaral, G. Dawson, & D. H. Geschwind (Eds.), *Autism spectrum disorders* (pp. 690–704). New York, NY: Oxford University Press, Inc.

Chen, F. S., & Johnson, S. C. (2012). An oxytocin receptor gene variant predicts attachment anxiety in females and autism-spectrum traits in males. *Social Psychological and Personality Science, 3*(1), 93–99. doi:10.1177/1948550611410325

Constantino, J. N. (2002). *The social responsiveness scale*. Los Angeles, CA: Western Psychological Services.
Constantino, J. N. (2011a). The quantitative nature of autistic social impairment. *Pediatric Research, 69*(5, Pt. 2), 55R–62R. doi:10.1203/PDR.0b013e318212ec6e
Constantino, J. N. (2011b). Autism as a quantitative trait. In D. G. Amaral, G. Dawson, & D. H. Geschwind (Eds.), *Autism spectrum disorders* (pp. 510–520). New York, NY: Oxford University Press.
Constantino, J. N., & Gruber, C. P. (2005). *The social responsiveness scale manual*. Los Angeles, CA: Western Psychological Services.
Constantino, J. N., & Todd, R. D. (2003). Autistic traits in the general population: A twin study. *Archives of General Psychiatry, 60*(5), 524–530. doi:10.1001/archpsyc.60.5.524
Constantino, J. N., Zhang, Y., Frazier, T., Abbacchi, A. M., & Law, P. (2010). Sibling recurrence and the genetic epidemiology of autism. *American Journal of Psychiatry, 167*(11), 1349–1356. doi:10.1176/appi.ajp.2010.09101470
Copy number variation. (2008). The new genetic frontier. *Harvard Mental Health Letter, 25*(4), 6–7.
Davidson, J., Goin-Kochel, R. P., Green-Snyder, L. A., Hundley, R. J., Warren, Z., & Peters, S. U. (2012). Expression of the broad autism phenotype in simplex autism families from the Simons Simplex Collection. *Journal of Autism and Developmental Disorders*. (Online publication). doi:10.1007/s10803-012-1492-1
Dawson, G., Estes, A., Munson, J., Schellenberg, G., Bernier, R., & Abbott, R. (2007). Quantitative assessment of autism symptom-related traits in probands and parents: Broader Phenotype Autism Symptom Scale. *Journal of Autism and Developmental Disorders, 37*(3), 523–536. doi:10.1007/s10803-006-0182-2
Denckla, M. B., & Rudel, R. G. (1976). Rapid "automatized" naming (R.A.N.): Dyslexia differentiated from other learning disabilities. *Neuropsychologia, 14*(4), 471–479.
Duvall, J. A., Lu, A., Cantor, R. M., Todd, R. D., Constantino, J. N., & Geschwind, D. H. (2007). A quantitative trait locus analysis of social responsiveness in multiplex autism families. *American Journal of Psychiatry, 164*(4), 656–662. doi:10.1176/appi.ajp.164.4.656
Eapen, V. (2011). Genetic basis of autism: Is there a way forward? *Current Opinion in Psychiatry, 24*(3), 226–236. doi:10.1097/YCO.0b013e328345927e
Ekman, P., & Friesen, W. V. (1975). *Pictures of facial affect*. Palo Alto, CA: Consulting Psychologists Press.
Fiorentini, C., Gray, L., Rhodes, G., Jeffery, L., & Pellicano, E. (2012). Reduced face identity aftereffects in relatives of children with autism. *Neuropsychologia, 50*, 2926–2932. doi:10.1016/j.neuropsychologia.2012.08.019
Fischbach, G. D., & Lord, C. (2010). The Simons Simplex Collection: A resource for identification of autism genetic risk factors. *Neuron, 68*(2), 192–195. doi:10.1016/j.neuron.2010.10.006
Folstein, S., & Rutter, M. (1977). Infantile autism: A genetic study of 21 twin pairs. *Journal of Child Psychology and Psychiatry, 18*(4), 297–321. doi:10.1111/j.1469-7610.1977.tb00443.x
Freitag, C. M. (2007). The genetics of autistic disorders and its clinical relevance: A review of the literature. *Molecular Psychiatry, 12*(1), 2–22. doi:10.1038/sj.mp.4001896
Gallagher, H., Happé, F., Brunswick, N., Fletcher, P., Frith, U., & Frith, C. (2000). Reading in the mind cartoons and stories: An fMRI study of 'theory of mind' in verbal and non-verbal tasks. *Neuropsychologia, 38*(1), 11–21. doi:10.1016/S0028-3932(99)00053-6

Geschwind, D. H. (2011). Genetics of autism spectrum disorders. *Trends in Cognitive Sciences*, *15*(9), 409–416. doi:10.1016/j.tics.2011.07.003
Ghaziuddin, M. (1997). Autism in Down syndrome: Family history correlates. *Journal of Intellectual Disability Research*, *41*(Pt. 1), 87–91. doi:10.1111/j.1365-2788.1997.tb00681.x
Ghaziuddin, M. (2000). Autism in down syndrome: A family history study. *Journal of Intellectual Disability Research*, *41*(Pt. 5), 562–566. doi:10.1046/j.1365-2788.2000.00271.x
Hertz-Picciotto, I., Croen, L. A., Hansen, R., Jones, C. R., van de Water, J., & Pessah, I. N. (2006). The CHARGE study: An epidemiologic investigation of genetic and environmental factors contributing to autism. *Environmental Health Perspectives*, *114*(7), 1119–1125. doi:10.1289/ehp.8483
Hoekstra, R. A., Bartels, M., Verweij, C. J. H., & Boomsma, D. I. (2007). Heritability of autistic traits in the general population. *Archives of Pediatrics and Adolescent Medicine*, *161*(4), 372–377. doi:10.1001/archpedi.161.4.372
Hurley, R. S. E., Losh, M., Parlier, M., Reznick, J. S., & Piven, J. (2007). The broad autism phenotype questionnaire. *Journal of Autism and Developmental Disorders*, *37*(9), 1679–1690. doi:10.1007/s10803-006-0299-3
International Molecular Genetic Study of Autism Consortium. (2000). *Family history interview: Interviewer impressions*. Unpublished interviewer impressions for autism.
Jensen, R. A. (2013). The background genetic effect of the genes underlying the broad autism phenotype as a unifying feature in gene × gene and gene × environment causal mechanisms in autism. *OA Autism*, *1*(2), 11–18. Retrieved from http://www.oapublishinglondon.com/images/article/pdf/1379116999.pdf
Kocovska, E., Fernell, E., Billstedt, E., Minnis, H., & Gillberg, C. (2012). Vitamin D and autism: Clinical review. *Research in Developmental Disabilities*, *33*(5), 1541–1550. doi:10.1016/j.ridd.2012.02.015
Lainhart, J. E., Ozonoff, S., Coon, H., Krasny, L., Dinh, E., Nice, J., & McMahon, W. (2002). Autism, regression, and the broader autism phenotype. *American Journal of Medical Genetics*, *113*(3), 231–237. doi:10.1002/ajmg.10615
Landa, R., Piven, J., Wzorek, M. M., Gayle, J. O., Chase, G. A., & Folstein, S. E. (1992). Social language use in parents of autistic individuals. *Psychological Medicine*, *22*(1), 245–254. doi:10.1017/S0033291700032918
Le Couteur, A., Bailey, A., Goode, S., Pickles, A., Robertson, S., Gottesman, I., & Rutter, M. (1996). A broader phenotype of autism: The clinical spectrum in twins. *Journal of Child Psychology and Psychiatry*, *37*(7), 785–801.
Lord, C., Rutter, M., & Le Couteur, A. (1994). Autism diagnostic interview-revised: A revised version of a diagnostic interview for caregivers of individuals with possible pervasive developmental disorders. *Journal of Autism and Developmental Disorders*, *24*(5), 659–685. doi:10.1007/BF02172145
Losh, M., Adolphs, R., & Piven, J. (2011). The broad autism phenotype. In D. G. Amaral, G. Dawson, & D. H. Geschwind (Eds.), *Autism spectrum disorders* (pp. 457–476). New York, NY: Oxford University Press, Inc.
Losh, M., Childress, D., Lam, K., & Piven, J. (2008a). Defining key features of the broad autism phenotype: A comparison across parents of multiple- and single-incidence autism families. *American Journal of Medical Genetics Part B: Neuropsychiatric Genetics*, *147B*(4), 424–433. doi:10.1002/ajmg.b.30612
Losh, M., Esserman, D., & Piven, J. (2010). Rapid automatized naming as an index of genetic liability to autism. *Journal of Neurodevelopmental Disorders*, *2*(2), 109–116. doi:10.1007/s11689-010-9045-4

Losh, M., Klusek, J., Martin, G. E., Sideris, J., Parlier, M., & Piven, J. (2012). Defining genetically meaningful language and personality traits in relatives of individuals with fragile X syndrome and relatives of individuals with autism. *American Journal of Medical Genetics, Part B: Neuropsychiatric Genetics, 159B*(6), 660–668. doi:10.1002/ajmg.b.32070

Losh, M., & Piven, J. (2007). Social-cognition and the broad autism phenotype: Identifying genetically meaningful phenotypes. *Journal of Child Psychology and Psychiatry, 48*(1), 105–112. doi:10.1111/j.1469-7610.2006.01594.x

Losh, M., Sullivan, P. F., Trembath, D., & Piven, J. (2008b). Current developments in the genetics of autism: From phenome to genome. *Journal of Neuropathology and Experimental Neurology, 67*(9), 829–837. doi:10.1097/NEN.0b013e318184482d

Marco, E. J., & Skuse, D. H. (2006). Autism – Lessons from the X chromosome. *Scan, 1*, 183–193. doi:10.1093/scan/nsl028

Newshaffer, C. J., Croen, L. A., Daniels, J., Giarelli, E., Grether, J. K., Levy, S. E., ... Windham, G. C. (2007). The epidemiology of autism spectrum disorders. *Annual Review of Public Health, 28*, 235–258. doi:10.1146/annurev.publhealth.28.021406.144007

Nyden, A., Hagberg, B., Gousse, V., & Rastam, M. (2011). A cognitive endophenotype of autism in families with multiple incidences. *Research in Autism Spectrum Disorders, 5*(1), 191–200. doi:10.1016/j.ras.2010.03.010

Piven, J. (1999). Genetic liability for autism: The behavioural expression in relatives. *International Review of Psychiatry, 11*(4), 299–308. doi:10.1080/09540269974186

Piven, J. (2002). Genetics of personality: The example of the broad autism phenotype. In J. Benjamin, R. P. Ebstein, & R. H. Belmaker (Eds.), *Molecular genetics and the human personality* (pp. 43–62). Washington, DC: American Psychiatric Publishing, Inc.

Piven, J., Palmer, P., Jacobi, D., Childress, D., & Arndt, S. (1997a). Broader autism phenotype: Evidence from a family history study of multiple-incidence autism families. *American Journal of Psychiatry, 154*(2), 185–190.

Piven, J., Palmer, P., Landa, R., Santangelo, S., Jacobi, D., & Childress, D. (1997b). Personality and language characteristics in parents from multiple-incidence autism families. *American Journal of Medical Genetics Part B: Neuropsychiatric Genetics, 74*(4), 398–411. doi:10.1002/(SICI)1096-8628(19970725)74:4 < 398::AID-AJMG11 > 3.0.CO;2-D

Piven, J., Vieland, V. J., Parlier, M., Thompson, A., O'Conner, I., Woodbury-Smith, M., ... Szatmari, P. (2013). A molecular genetic study of autism and related phenotypes in extended pedigrees. *Journal of Neurodevelopmental Disorders, 5*, 30–44. (Open access article). Retrieved from http://www.jneurodevdisorders.com/content/5/1/30

Reitan, R. (1958). Validity of the trail making tests as an indicator of organic brain damage. *Perceptual and Motor Skills, 8*, 271–276.

Rutter, M., Bailey, A., & Lord, C. (2003). *SCQ: The Social Communication Questionnaire*. Los Angeles, CA: Western Psychological Services.

Santangelo, S. L., & Folstein, S. E. (1995). Social deficits in the families of autistic probands. *American Journal of Human Genetics, 57*(4 Suppl.), A20.

Saresella, M., Marventano, I., Guerini, F. R., Mancuso, R., Ceresa, L., Zanzottera, M., ... Clerici, M. (2009). An autistic endophenotype results in complex immune dysfunction in healthy siblings of autistic children. *Biological Psychiatry, 66*(10), 978–984. doi:10.1016/j.biopsych.2009.06.020

Sasson, N. J., Lam, K. S. L., Parlier, M., Daniels, J. L., & Piven, J. (2013). Autism and the broad autism phenotype: Familial and intergenerational transmission. *Journal of Neurodevelopmental Disorders, 5*(1), 11. (Open access article). doi:10.1186/1866-1955-5-11

Shallice, T. (1982). Specific impairments of planning. *Philosophical Transactions of the Royal Society of London, 298*, 199–209.

Shelton, J. F., Hertz-Picciotto, I., & Pessah, I. N. (2012). Tipping the balance of autism risk: Potential mechanisms linking pesticides and autism. *Environmental Health Perspectives, 120*(7), 944–951. doi:10.1289/ehp.1104553

Spence, S. J. (2004). The genetics of autism. *Seminars in Pediatric Neurology, 11*(3), 196–204. doi:10.1016/j.spen.2004.07.003

Spencer, M. D., Holt, R. J., Chura, L. R., Calder, A. J., Suckling, J., Bullmore, E. T., & Baron-Cohen, S. (2012). Atypical activation during the embedded figures task as a functional magnetic resonance imaging endophenotype of autism. *Brain, 135*, 3469–3480. doi:10.1093/brain/aws229

Spencer, M. D., Holt, R. J., Chura, L. R., Suckling, J., Calder, A. J., Bullmore, E. T., & Baron-Cohen, S. (2011). A novel functional brain imaging endophenotype of autism: The neural response to facial expression of emotion. *Translational Psychiatry, 1*, e19. doi:10.1038/tp.2011.18

St. Pourcain, B., Wang, K., Glessner, J. T., Golding, J., Steer, C., Ring, S. M., ... Smith, G. D. (2010). Association between a high-risk autism locus on 5p14 and social communication spectrum phenotypes in the general population. *American Journal of Psychiatry, 167*(11), 1364–1372. doi:10.1176/appi.ajp.2010.09121789

Starr, E., Berument, S. K., Pickles, A., Tomlins, M., Bailey, A., Papanikolaou, K., & Rutter, M. (2001). A family genetic study of autism associated with profound mental retardation. *Journal of Autism and Developmental Disorders, 31*(1), 89–96. doi:10.1023/A:1005669915105

Steyaert, J. G., & De La Marche, W. (2008). What's new in autism? *European Journal of Pediatrics, 167*(10), 1091–1101. doi:10.1007/s00431-008-0764-4

Sucksmith, E., Roth, I., & Hoekstra, R. A. (2011). Autistic traits below the clinical threshold: Re-examining the broader autism phenotype in the 21st century. *Neuropsychology Review, 21*(4), 360–389. doi:10.1007/s11065-011-9183-9

Sung, Y. J., Dawson, G., Munson, J., Estes, A., Schellenberg, G. D., & Wijsman, E. M. (2005). Genetic investigation of quantitative traits related to autism: Use of multivariate polygenic models with ascertainment adjustment. *American Journal of Human Genetics, 76*(1), 68–81. doi:10.1086/426951

Tyrer, P. (1988). Personality assessment schedule. In P. Tyrer (Ed.), *Personality disorders: Diagnosis, management, and course* (pp. 51–100). London: Butterworth and Company.

Vincent, J. B., Melmer, G., Bolton, P. F., Hodgkinson, S., Holmes, D., Curtis, D., & Gurling, H. M. (2005). Genetic linkage analysis of the X chromosome in autism, with emphasis on the fragile X region. *Psychiatric Genetics, 15*(2), 83–90.

Virkud, Y. V., Todd, R. D., Abbacchi, A. M., Zhang, Y., & Constantino, J. N. (2008). Familial aggregation of quantitative autistic traits in multiplex versus simplex autism. *American Journal of Medical Genetics Part B: Neuropsychiatric Genetics, 150B*(3), 328–334. doi:10.1002/ajmg.b.30810

Volk, H. E., Hertz-Picciotto, I., Delwiche, L., Lurmann, F., & McConnell, R. (2011). Residential proximity to freeways and autism in the CHARGE study. *Environmental Health Perspectives, 119*(6), 873–877. doi:10.1289/ehp.1002835

Whitbourne, S. K., & Halgin, R. P. (2014). *Abnormal psychology: Clinical perspectives on psychological disorders* (7th ed., DSM-5 update). New York, NY: McGraw-Hill Education.
Williams, D. M., & Bowler, D. M. (2014). Autism spectrum disorder: Fractionable or coherent? *Autism, 18*(1), 2–5. doi:10.1177/1362361313513523
Witkin, H. A., Oltman, P. K., Raskin, E., & Karp, S. (1971). *A manual for the embedded figures test*. Palo Alto, CA: Consulting Psychologists Press.

CHAPTER 4

OTHER BIOLOGICAL ASPECTS OF THE BROAD AUTISM PHENOTYPE

This chapter presents information about other biological characteristics of the broad autism phenotype (BAP). The chapter is divided into three sections. Sections 4.1 and 4.2 focus on differences in brain anatomical structure and function. Section 4.3 examines the relationship between head circumference and the BAP. Section 4.4 examines immune system functioning and the BAP.

4.1. DIFFERENCES IN BRAIN STRUCTURE

Although no universally accepted definition of the BAP currently exists (Mandy, Charman, Puura, & Skuse, 2014), most would agree that it includes mild impairments in social functioning and pragmatic language (Pelphrey, Adolphs, & Morris, 2004), as well as the personality features of aloofness and rigidity (Belger, Carpenter, Yucel, Cleary, & Donkers, 2011). A review article by Dawson et al. (2002) identified brain structures believed to underlie these and other characteristics of the BAP. One core facet of the BAP involves subtle deficits in social cognition; these deficits are associated with the amygdala and the ventromedial prefrontal cortex. Another key characteristic of the BAP is mild difficulty with language; such difficulties are linked to the superior temporal gyrus, the temporoparietal cortex, and Broca's area. Minor problems with planning, flexibility, and other executive functions of the brain also may be an aspect of the BAP; differences in the prefrontal cortex contribute to these kinds of dysfunctions. Alterations in face processing that have been observed in the BAP are supposedly due to variations in the fusiform gyrus, superior temporal sulcus, and amygdala. In addition, the BAP includes differences in declarative memory that are presumably due to alterations in the hippocampus and prefrontal cortex. Lastly, mild impairment in the ability to imitate movements may be a feature of the BAP; if so, such ability would be associated with the superior temporal sulcus, Broca's area, and the inferior parietal cortex (Dawson et al., 2002).

Belmonte et al. (2004) also highlighted the prefrontal cortex, as well as the medial temporal lobe, as having potential relevance for the BAP. They hypothesized that abnormal connections between these areas of the brain may lead to overactivation of sensory inputs, thereby contributing to problems with visual attention. Belmonte and colleagues (2004) further reported that unaffected brothers of people with autism spectrum disorders (ASD) demonstrate low levels of activation in these brain regions, similar to what is seen among individuals with ASD. Consequently these authors suggested that unusual patterns of brain organization involving "local overconnectivity and long-range underconnectivity" (p. 9229) might be an endophenotype that signals an increased risk for ASD.

In a more recent article, Barnea-Goraly, Lotspeich, and Reiss (2010) examined white matter structure in the brains of children with autism and their non-ASD siblings. White matter underlies the gray neurons of the cerebral cortex and consists of "aggregations of myelinated and non-myelinated axons linking different cortical and subcortical regions" (Mills et al., 2013, p. 2). According to Barnea-Goraly et al., white matter structure is "an important aspect of brain connectivity" (p. 1053). Prior investigations had shown that white matter structure is abnormal in the brains of children with autism. Therefore, Barnea-Goraly and associates sought to learn whether such abnormalities also might be present in siblings' brains. Using diffusion tensor imaging, they scanned the brains of 13 children with ASD, 13 siblings who were sex-matched to the participants with ASD, and 11 neurotypical children. The mean full-scale intelligence quotient (IQ) score of the ASD group was significantly lower than the mean IQ score for both the sibling group and the control group; however, no significant differences existed among the three groups in terms of mean age. Results of the Barnea-Goraly et al. (2010) inquiry revealed that there were no significant differences in white matter structure between the ASD group members and their siblings. However, the white matter structure of both of these groups differed significantly from that of the typically developing participants. In comparison to the control group, both the ASD group and the siblings group showed noteworthy differences in white matter in the medial prefrontal and temporoparietal areas of the brain, including brain regions that are involved in social cognition, face processing, and theory of mind. On the basis of these findings, Barnea-Goraly et al. surmised that alterations in the brain's white matter structure might be a biomarker of risk for the development of ASD.

Unaffected siblings of individuals with ASD also appear to have reduced volume in the amygdala when compared to typically developing controls (Dalton, Nacewicz, Alexander, & Davidson, 2007). Regarding other structural differences in the brains of first-degree relatives of people with ASD, Lainhart and Lange (2011) reported the following. When compared with parents of typically developing children, parents of children with ASD have been found to have more gray matter volume in the frontal, parietal, temporal, and occipital lobes of the brain. The ASD literature also mentions larger volume in the left hippocampus of ASD parents versus control parents (Gerdts & Bernier, 2011; Lainhart & Lange, 2011; Rojas et al., 2011).

To summarize, current research on brain structure suggests that the BAP involves structural differences in the prefrontal cortex, amygdala, hippocampus, Broca's area, and other regions located in the temporal and parietal lobes. Differences in white matter structure also appear to be associated with the BAP.

4.2. DIFFERENCES IN BRAIN FUNCTION

Not only differences in brain structure but also variations in brain function have been considered in relation to the BAP. Because infant siblings of children with ASD constitute a group that is known to be at risk for either the BAP or ASD (Christensen et al., 2010; Newshaffer et al., 2012), two recent studies (Holmboe et al., 2010; Lloyd-Fox et al., 2013) examined brain function in this population.

Holmboe et al. (2010) studied the functioning of the frontal cortex in a group of 31 infants in the age range of 9–10 months old, all of whom had an older brother or sister who was formally diagnosed with ASD. The researchers compared these youngsters to a control group comprised of 33 typically developing infants in the 9–10 months age range, all of whom had no family history of ASD. Babies in this experiment were given a selective attention task while seated on a parent's lap. Each infant was shown a series of cartoon stimuli in the center of a screen in front of them; half of these stimuli were interesting cartoons, and half of them were repetitious and uninteresting. Once it was clear that a baby was looking at the central image, a distractor image appeared on the screen either to the left or right of center, and at an angle in relation to the central stimulus. The babies' eye movements were tracked and recorded to determine how long it took for them to disengage from the central image and look at the peripheral distractor. Results indicated that some of the ASD siblings had trouble shifting their visual focus away from the center image and toward the peripheral distractor. In comparison to the neurotypical infants, the ASD siblings also failed to focus longer on interesting stimuli than on boring stimuli. Because visual attention and inhibition are controlled by the frontal cortex, Holmboe et al. suggested that they had detected "atypical frontal cortex functioning in the infant broader autism phenotype" (p. 482).

High-risk infants also participated in a 2013 study by Lloyd-Fox et al., who investigated the role of the temporal lobe in processing social stimuli. Eighteen babies who were 4–6 months old, and who had an older biological sibling with ASD, made up the experimental group for this study. Sixteen infants of similar age and with no family history of ASD served in the control group. This team of scientists conducted functional near-infrared spectroscopy to scan regions of the temporal lobe, looking for activation in response to visual and auditory social stimuli. Visual stimuli in this study consisted of videos of women who either moved their eyes from side to side or played children's hand games (e.g., peek-a-boo). At varying times during the videos, the infants also were given auditory stimuli, some of which were social and some of which were not. Social auditory stimuli consisted of adult voices that coughed, laughed, cried, or yawned; nonsocial auditory stimuli included sounds that would be familiar to babies such as a rattle, a squeaky toy, or running water. Visual and auditory stimuli were not synchronized. Lloyd-Fox and associates observed that in comparison to the typically developing infants, babies with ASD siblings showed less response to both visual and auditory social stimuli. These researchers noted that the group differences were not due to differences in age, head size, or time spent looking at visual stimuli. They asserted that "some infants at risk for autism may show a lack of cortical specialization to social stimuli within the first 6 months of life" (p. 6), and speculated that these atypical patterns of brain functioning might be an indicator of either future ASD or the BAP (Lloyd-Fox et al., 2013).

Older siblings of people with ASD also have been the focus of studies regarding differences in brain function that may be associated with the BAP. During an inquiry conducted by Dalton et al. (2007), 21 individuals with ASD, 12 of their siblings, and 19 control participants underwent functional magnetic resonance imaging (fMRI) while they engaged in a facial recognition task. Dalton and colleagues discovered that both the ASD group and the sibling group manifested significantly less activation in the right posterior fusiform gyrus when looking at photographs of faces. Therefore, the authors proposed that the BAP involves variations in brain circuitry related to social processing.

Another investigation by Floris et al. (2013) looked at asymmetry in the brains of 40 adolescent males with ASD, 40 of their unaffected biological siblings, and 40 neurotypical control participants. Floris et al. (2013) were particularly interested in the corpus callosum, due to previous research which had reported reductions in the size of the corpus callosum among people with ASD. In this study, participants with ASD manifested stronger lateralization toward the right hemisphere (RH) of the brain in the posterior and anterior midbody sections of the corpus callosum. However, the researchers did not obtain significant differences between the sibling group and the control group. As a result, they determined that "cerebral lateralization does not appear to be a marker of familial risk for" ASD (Floris et al., 2013, p. 1768).

In addition to siblings, parents of children with ASD comprise another group whose members may meet criteria for the BAP. Studies have been conducted to investigate the brain function of parents whose children have ASD, as compared to adults with no family history of ASD. For example, Baron-Cohen et al. (2006) recruited a sample of 12 neurotypical adults as well as 6 fathers and 6 mothers of children with ASD. All of these participants were similar in intelligence and socioeconomic status. They completed the Adult Embedded Figures Task (EFT; Witkin, Dyk, Faterson, Goodenough, & Karp, 1962) to evaluate brain function when making visual-spatial judgments, and the Eyes Test (Baron-Cohen, Wheelwright, Hill, Raste, & Plumb, 2001a) to examine their ability to recognize emotions in photographs showing only the eyes portion of a face. While completing these assessments, they also were given fMRI scans. Scans taking during the EFT revealed no differences between mothers and fathers of children with ASD; however, both of these groups manifested less activity in the extrastriate cortex than the sex-matched control participants. When considering scans that were completed during the Eyes Test, both mothers and fathers of children with ASD exhibited greater brain activity in the left inferior frontal gyrus than the sex-matched controls did. Based on these findings, Baron-Cohen and colleagues (2006) decided that parents of children with ASD evince unusual patterns of brain functioning that suggest "hyper-masculinization of the brain" (p. 122). However, they cautioned that their results should be considered only preliminary due to the small size of their participant sample, as well as the lack of age-matching between ASD parents and controls in this study.

Brain functions that underlie the capacity for empathy were the focus of a study by Greimel and associates in 2010. These researchers solicited four groups of participants for their investigation: 15 adolescent males with ASD, 11 of their fathers, 15 neurotypical teenaged males, and 9 of their fathers. All of the adolescents were right-handed and were equivalent with regard to age and overall intellectual functioning. Similarly, the fathers were comparable in terms of handedness, age, and intelligence. Fathers completed the Autism Spectrum Quotient (AQ; Baron-Cohen, Wheelwright, Skinner, Martin, & Clubley, 2001b) to check for the possible presence of ASD. Those who had children with ASD obtained higher AQ scores, with two of them exceeding the clinical cutoff score.

To assess the empathic abilities of the adolescent participants, Greimel et al. (2010) had all of the fathers complete a rating scale called the Griffith Empathy Measure (Dadds et al., 2008). This test examines both cognitive and emotional aspects of empathy. According to the fathers' ratings of their sons, the teens with ASD were rated as being much less empathic than their counterparts in the control group. In like fashion, all fathers completed a self-report questionnaire called the Balanced Emotional Empathy Scale (BEES; Mehrabian, 1997). Fathers whose sons had ASD rated themselves as less empathic in comparison to the BEES scores of fathers in the control group (Greimel et al., 2010).

Participants in the Greimel et al. (2010) study were shown a series of happy, sad, and neutral faces. The adolescents were shown boys' faces, while the fathers viewed faces of adult men. They were asked to infer the emotional state of the face being shown, as well as their own emotional state in response to each face. All participants underwent fMRI scans while viewing the facial stimuli. Greimel et al. discovered no differences between the two groups of fathers in terms of performance on the emotion inference task. However, during this task, fathers of ASD teens displayed reduced activation in the anterior fusiform gyrus and amygdala, which resembled the brain activation patterns of their sons with ASD. This pattern held true even when the two fathers whose AQ scores had exceeded the clinical cutoff were excluded from analyses. Thus, it appears that reduced fusiform gyrus activation during an empathic reasoning task may be a marker of the BAP.

Rojas et al. (2011) studied the brain's gamma-band responses, generated by auditory stimuli in the range of 30–80 Hz, in parents of children with ASD. He and his colleagues already knew from previous studies that gamma-band oscillations in response to auditory stimuli are lower among people who have been diagnosed with ASD. This finding led them to wonder whether similar patterns might be found among first-degree relatives of individuals with ASD. The research team obtained a sample of 21 parents of children with ASD and a control group of 20 neurotypical adults. The two groups were similar with regard to numbers of men and women, age, socioeconomic status, and intellectual functioning. Magnetoencephalography recordings were taken while the participants were presented with auditory stimuli in both ears. Each stimulus consisted of 500 milliseconds of white noise at 32, 40, or 48 Hz, with 2-second intervals between each of the 150 separate stimulus trials. This study revealed that in comparison to the controls, the parents of children with ASD demonstrated reduced steady-state gamma-band responses in the left hemisphere of the brain. According to Rojas and associates, these findings were similar to those that previously had been obtained from children diagnosed with ASD. Therefore, they suggested that gamma-band deficits are related to the BAP and ASD (Rojas et al., 2011).

Because the general population may include individuals with ASD traits, Vladeanu, Monteith-Hodge, and Bourne (2012) investigated brain lateralization during facial emotion processing, using a convenience sample of adult students. These scientists were aware of earlier research indicating that men with Asperger syndrome exhibited a bias toward using the brain's RH to process facial emotions like happiness and sadness. This finding prompted them to speculate whether undiagnosed individuals who possessed ASD traits might display a similar pattern of brain activity. Vladeanu et al. recruited 32 men and 32 women attending a Scottish university, all of whom were right-handed, and had them complete the Broad Autism Phenotype Questionnaire (BAPQ; Hurley, Losh, Parlier, Reznick, & Piven, 2007). This measure provided a score for each of three subscales to examine the BAP characteristics of aloofness, rigidity, and pragmatic language deficits. Each participant also completed 24 trials of a so-called "chimeric faces test" (Vladeanu et al., 2012, p. 442) using facial pictures from a set originally created by Paul Ekman. The visual stimuli in the chimeric faces test were created by joining two vertical halves of a face; one half of the face depicted an emotion and the other half showed a neutral expression. For each trial, participants were shown a pair of chimeric faces and were asked to determine which of the two faces seemed to display the more intense emotional state. This method resembles a divided visual field test, in which "choosing the face with the emotion in the left visual field indicates RH dominance" (Vladeanu et al., 2012, p. 443) while choosing the face in the right visual field would signify dominant activity in the left hemisphere of the brain.

The visual trials in the Vladeanu et al. (2012) study included chimeric faces that displayed all of the basic emotions: anger, disgust, fear, happiness, sadness, and surprise. Analyses of results yielded no significant findings for female participants. Additionally, the BAP features of rigid personality and pragmatic language difficulties were not predictive of brain lateralization for emotion processing in male participants. However, regression analyses of data from the men in this study detected a relationship between aloof personality, as measured by the BAPQ, and brain lateralization for three emotions. Vladneanu and colleagues found that men who obtained high scores on the aloof personality subscale of the BAPQ relied more heavily on the RH when processing happiness, surprise, and fear. Zero-order correlational analyses also identified significant correlations between rigid personality and the emotions of fear and anger. Thus, the authors of this study hypothesized the existence of an interaction between ASD personality traits, emotion processing abilities, and the degree of brain hemisphere lateralization for processing emotions that are communicated through facial expressions. They noted that people with tendencies for social disinterest and rigidity may be likely to have stronger brain lateralization for emotion processing (Vladeanu et al., 2012).

On the basis of the above studies, the following assumptions can be made about the brain functioning of individuals with the BAP. Variations in their brain functioning appear to include atypical patterns of activity in the frontal cortex and aberrant cortical specialization for social stimuli. These differences manifest in the form of reduced activity in the amygdala, anterior fusiform gyrus, and right posterior fusiform gyrus when viewing human faces. In addition, the processing of facial emotions seems to be accompanied by increased activity in the left inferior frontal gyrus. Individuals with an aloof personality demonstrate increased RH lateralization when processing faces that display happiness, surprise, and fear. Other differences in brain functioning that relate to the BAP include a reduction of left hemisphere steady-state gamma-band responses to auditory stimuli, as well as diminished activity of the extrastriate cortex when making visual-spatial judgments.

4.3. DIFFERENCES IN HEAD CIRCUMFERENCE

Macrocephaly (i.e., increased head circumference) often has been reported as a characteristic of people with ASD. However, fewer studies have investigated whether differences in head circumference also are a consistent feature of the BAP. One such inquiry reported increased head size that met or surpassed the 97th percentile for more than 11% of people whose siblings had ASD, as well as for almost 19% of parents whose children had ASD (Fidler, Bailey, & Smalley, 2000). Another inquiry by Miles, Hadden, Takahashi, and Hillman (2000) specifically investigated head circumference in families containing a child with ASD. Among their sample of 32 individuals with ASD and macrocephaly, they found the BAP in 9.5% of all siblings. When limiting their inquiry to siblings who were born after the probands with macrocephaly, these researchers discovered that nearly 27% of those siblings fit the definition of the BAP. Additionally, Miles et al. examined the parents of children with ASD and found that while none of the parents had "overt autism" (p. 347), their average head circumference tended toward macrocephaly. These authors went so far as to suggest that non-ASD parents with macrocephaly "may be carrying a gene(s) that puts them at risk for having a child with autism" (Miles et al., 2000, p. 348). In 2002, Lainhart et al. conducted an investigation of the relationship between regressive ASD and the BAP. Within the context of their study, they noticed a significantly larger mean head circumference among mothers of children without regressive ASD, when compared to mothers of children with regressive ASD. However, rates of macrocephaly were not significantly different for these two groups of women.

According to the few studies mentioned in this section, it looks as though enlarged head circumference may be common among people with the BAP. This physical feature has been reported among both parents and siblings of individuals with ASD. It may signify that the brains of these individuals are larger than what is typical (Randolph-Gips & Srinivasan, 2012). Herbert (2005) referred to macrocephaly as an endophenotype for ASD. However, she drew a distinction between an endophenotype and a biomarker, cautioning that macrocephaly cannot be considered a biomarker of ASD for two reasons. First, macrocephaly occurs in 3% of the US population and can be found among many people who do not have ASD. Second, macrocephaly is not associated with ASD alone, but also can be observed in connection with attention deficit hyperactivity disorder (Herbert, 2005). Nevertheless, it appears reasonable to assume on the basis of the existing literature that many people who meet criteria for the BAP may exhibit either increased head circumference or full-fledged macrocephaly.

4.4. POSSIBLE DIFFERENCES IN IMMUNE SYSTEM FUNCTIONING

As discussed in Chapter 3, Saresella and colleagues (2009) suggested that differences in immunologic functioning might be a potential endophenotype for ASD. Therefore, it is not surprising to find several studies implying that autoimmune disorders may be more prevalent among individuals with the BAP. Comi, Zimmerman, Frye, Law, and Peeden (1999) were among the first to notice and report this phenomenon. Recognizing that many children with ASD have abnormalities in immune system functioning, Comi et al. surveyed 61 families of individuals with ASD and compared their responses to those of 46 neurotypical controls. They discovered that 46% of families of children with ASD had two or more members who suffered from an autoimmune disorder, while the same was true for only 26% of control participants. Of particular note, 16% of ASD cases in this study had mothers with an autoimmune disorder, as compared to only 2% of mothers in the control group. Also, 21% of first-degree relatives of ASD cases had an autoimmune disorder, but only 4% of first-degree relatives of the control group had such conditions.

Sweeten, Bowyer, Posey, Halberstadt, and McDougle (2003) conducted a follow-up of the study by Comi et al. (1999), including not two but three groups of participants. Similar to the earlier study, Sweeten et al. included families of children with ASD and families of neurotypical children. However, they also included a third group comprised of families of children with an autoimmune disorder. Participants in this investigation completed a 45-item self-report concerning first- and second-degree relatives who had been diagnosed with a variety of autoimmune conditions. These researchers hypothesized that the prevalence of autoimmune disorders among ASD families would fall between the prevalence rates of the other two participant groups. Instead, however, Sweeten et al. learned that rates of autoimmune disorders in the families of children with ASD significantly exceeded the rates found in both of the other groups. Parents of children with ASD, and mothers of these children in particular, reported the highest frequencies of autoimmune disorders in comparison to the parents of neurotypical children.

In most respects the above findings were similar to those of Comi et al. (1999), yet Sweeten and colleagues (2003) pointed out the following difference. The 1999 study found rheumatoid arthritis to be the most commonly reported autoimmune condition among its participants, whereas Sweeten et al. uncovered higher rates of hypothyroidism, Hashimoto's thyroiditis, and rheumatic fever in their sample. Although these scientists described their results as preliminary due to their reliance on questionnaire data, they expressed a belief that future researchers should continue to probe the connections between having a family member with ASD and having an autoimmune condition (Sweeten et al., 2003).

Similarly, Keil et al. (2010) sought to examine the relationship between ASD in children and autoimmune disorders in their parents. Using information from three Swedish registries, this team identified 1,227 cases of children with ASD. They also located 25 matched controls for each participant, for a total of 30,693 controls in their study. Analyses by Keil and colleagues revealed a weak connection between ASD in children and autoimmune disorders in parents. They observed a relationship between rheumatic fever and ASD when considering both mothers and fathers. Among mothers, other autoimmune conditions that also were correlated with ASD included type 1 diabetes, myasthenia gravis, and idiopathic thrombocytopenic purpura. These authors noted that while autoimmune disorders occur infrequently, children in their study whose parents had an autoimmune disorder were almost 50% more likely to be diagnosed with ASD by 10 years of age (Keil et al., 2010).

In the three studies discussed above, the possibility exists that at least some of the parents whose children had ASD might meet criteria for the BAP. Therefore, these investigations suggest a potential link between the BAP and autoimmune disorders. However, other research presents a different picture. For example, Micali, Chakrabarti, and Fombonne (2004) used data from an epidemiological survey in the United Kingdom to examine family histories of autoimmune diseases among the parents of 79 children with ASD as compared to parents of 61 typically developing children. Data were available for 79 mothers and 73 fathers of children with ASD, and for 59 mothers and 51 fathers of neurotypical children. A trend toward having arthritis was reported among the ASD parents, but this trend failed to reach statistical significance. Separate analyses by gender for any autoimmune disorders also were nonsignificant; rates of autoimmune disorder were similar in both the ASD and control parent groups.

Croen, Grether, Yoshida, Odouli, and Van de Water (2005) looked at autoimmune diseases specifically in mothers of children with ASD. They obtained information from the Kaiser Permanente outpatient clinic databases regarding mothers of children born between January of 1995 and June of 1999. For every child who had ASD, these researchers included five randomly selected children who had not been diagnosed with ASD. Croen and colleagues discerned that mothers from both groups of children had comparable rates of autoimmune disease. Upon conducting further analyses, the only autoimmune disorder that was found to be significantly linked to ASD was psoriasis. The research team concluded that maternal autoimmune disorders were not likely to significantly increase the risk of ASD in offspring. However, they also wrote, "... our observation that these conditions were more strongly associated with autism in families with more than 1 ASD-affected child may suggest that genes underlying atopy may also be etiologically related to autism" (Croen et al., 2005, p. 155). *Atopy* refers to an allergic condition, believed to be of hereditary origin, which leads to asthma, hives, or hay fever when the affected person is exposed to antigens in the environment (Merriam-Webster, 2014).

Valicenti-McDermott et al. (2006) conducted a cross-sectional study to learn whether gastrointestinal (GI) problems in children with ASD were associated with a family history of autoimmune disorders. Using a structured interview, they gathered information about 50 children with ASD, 50 children with other forms of developmental disorder, and 50 neurotypical youngsters. GI disturbances were significantly more common among children with ASD in comparison to the other two groups, but there was no connection between family history of autoimmune disease and GI symptoms in children with ASD. This research team also asked about the presence of autoimmune conditions in first- or second-degree relatives of the participants, and indicated that "there was no difference in the reported prevalence of family histories of autoimmune diseases among the 3 groups" (Valicenti-McDermott et al., 2006, p. S133).

Yet another study by Mouridsen, Rich, Isager, and Nedergaard (2007) investigated the connection between autoimmune disorders in parents and ASD in children. The data set for this inquiry came from the Danish National Hospital Register and spanned an observational time frame of 27 years. Mouridsen and associates screened parents of 111 children with ASD for 35 different autoimmune disorders. The comparison group in this study consisted of a matched group of parents of 330 typically developing children. Rates of autoimmune disorders were almost twice as high among fathers of children with ASD in comparison to fathers of neurotypical children, although rates of autoimmune conditions were similar in both groups of mothers. Mouridsen et al. identified two autoimmune diseases that were significantly related to ASD: type 1 diabetes among fathers, and ulcerative colitis among mothers. Nevertheless, these authors concluded that in general, their data did not imply an association between autoimmune diseases in parents and ASD in children.

Among the four studies that were just discussed, only the investigation by Micali et al. (2004) explicitly looked at the BAP. The other three studies included data from parents, some of whom might be likely to have BAP features. Findings from these four studies do not appear to support the premise that persons with the BAP may be more likely than the general population to suffer from autoimmune diseases. Taken as a whole, the results of research about a link between the BAP and autoimmune disorders are inconsistent. Thus, more studies are needed before it can be known whether autoimmune disorders truly are more prevalent among people who exhibit the BAP.

4.5. OTHER BIOLOGICAL DIFFERENCES IN THE BAP

In addition to the factors already mentioned in this chapter, various other biological differences have been reportedly connected to the BAP. One of the earliest such differences mentioned in the literature is elevated levels of serotonin in the blood of parents and siblings of children with ASD. A review article by Bailey, Palferman, Heavey, and Le Couteur (1998) indicated that relatives of "hyperserotonergic" individuals with ASD (p. 387) also manifested higher levels of whole blood serotonin. A later review article by Goussé et al. (2002) claimed that "serotonin has been the most investigated biological marker among relatives of autistic subjects" (p. 124). Goussé and colleagues cited several studies whose results found heightened levels of serotonin among mothers, fathers, and siblings of children with ASD. These authors posited that higher whole blood serotonin levels might be related to genetic risk for ASD (Goussé et al., 2002).

Micali et al. (2004) listed several medical problems that parents of children with ASD endorsed. Asthma, arthritis, eczema, psoriasis, irritable bowel disease, and type 1 diabetes were autoimmune disorders that parents reported in this study. Additionally, some parents indicated hypertension, migraine headaches, and neurological conditions such as multiple sclerosis and epilepsy. However, the latter condition may be rare among individuals with the BAP; Rutter (2011) claimed that BAP is not associated with epilepsy.

A few factors concerning human reproduction also have been cited in relation to the BAP. For example, Eriksson, Westerlund, Anderlid, Gillberg, and Fernell (2012) speculated that being an older father when one's first child is born might be associated with the BAP. According to Lundstrom et al. (2010), one possibility is that "autistic-like traits in the parents might delay reproduction" (p. 854). However, another study (Puleo, Reichenberg, Smith, Kryzak, & Silverman, 2008) disputed this notion, instead asserting that as men age, their sperm cells are more likely to contain de novo mutations that are transmitted to their offspring.

With regard to pregnancy and birth, Zwaigenbaum and colleagues (2002) explored the relationship between the BAP and obstetric complications. They obtained a sample of 60 families that contained 78 children with ASD and 88 unaffected siblings. By administering a standardized interview to the children's mothers, the researchers learned whether the gestational periods and births of the children included any complications. This group of investigators also administered the Family History Interview (Bolton et al., 1994) to parents as well as grandparents, aunts, and uncles from both sides of the children's families, to assess for the BAP in second- and third-degree relatives of the children. Zwaigenbaum et al. discovered that families with a higher loading for the BAP had higher rates of obstetric complications among the unaffected siblings. They concluded that minor complications during pregnancy and birth "may relate to familial factors that lead to expression of milder autism-like features in other relatives" (Zwaigenbaum et al., 2002, p. 578).

Differences in testosterone levels also may be relevant to the BAP. Simon Baron-Cohen's (2002) androgen theory of ASD proposes that ASD may result from elevated levels of fetal testosterone. Based on this theory, Ingudomnukul, Baron-Cohen, Wheelwright, and Knickmeyer (2007) hypothesized that mothers of children with ASD might have the BAP and therefore might be more likely to experience medical conditions stemming from elevated testosterone. They surveyed 54 women with ASD, 74 mothers of children with ASD, and 183 mothers of neurotypical children, asking them whether they had a variety of testosterone-related medical issues. According to results of their inquiry, mothers of children with ASD were more likely than mothers in the control group to have a history of severe acne and abnormal growths, tumors, or cancers of the breast and uterus. Therefore, Ingudomnukul et al. assumed that people with the BAP may exhibit higher levels of testosterone in adulthood, but they cautioned that this finding needed replication and further study.

4.6. SUMMARY

Findings of recent studies reveal that the BAP involves a variety of biological features that differ from what is found among the general populace. These include structural differences in both cortical and subcortical regions of the brain, which in turn may be linked to atypical activity in the frontal cortex and in areas of the brain that are responsible for the processing of social stimuli. Other commonly occurring biological aspects of the BAP include increases in head circumference, levels of whole blood serotonin and testosterone, and rates of obstetric complications. Some studies also have suggested that autoimmune disorders and epilepsy may be associated with the BAP, but current research is inconclusive regarding the association between these conditions and the BAP.

REFERENCES

Bailey, A., Palferman, S., Heavey, L., & Le Couteur, A. (1998). Autism: The phenotype in relatives. *Journal of Autism and Developmental Disorders, 28*(5), 369–392. doi:l10.1023/A:1026048320785

Barnea-Goraly, N., Lotspeich, L. J., & Reiss, A. L. (2010). Similar white matter aberrations in children with autism and their unaffected siblings. *Archives of General Psychiatry, 67*(10), 1052–1060. doi:10.1001/archgenpsychiatry.2010.123

Baron-Cohen, S. (2002). The extreme male brain theory of autism. *Trends in Cognitive Sciences, 6*(6), 248–254. doi:10.1016/S1364-6613(02)01904-06

Baron-Cohen, S., Ring, H., Chitnis, X., Wheelwright, S., Gregory, L., Williams, S., ... Bullmore, E. (2006). fMRI of parents of children with Asperger syndrome: A pilot study. *Brain and Cognition, 61*(1), 122–130. doi:10.1016/j.bandc.2005.12.011

Baron-Cohen, S., Wheelwright, S., Hill, J., Raste, Y., & Plumb, I. (2001a). The 'Reading the Mind in the Eyes' Test revised version: A study of normal adults, and adults with Asperger syndrome or high-functioning autism. *Journal of Child Psychology and Psychiatry, 42*(2), 241–252. doi:10.1111/1469-7610.00715

Baron-Cohen, S., Wheelwright, S., Skinner, R., Martin, J., & Clubley, E. (2001b). The Autism Spectrum Quotient (AQ): Evidence from Asperger syndrome/high-functioning autism, males and females, scientists and mathematicians. *Journal of Autism and Developmental Disorders, 31*(1), 5–17. doi:10.1023/A:1005653411471

Belger, A., Carpenter, K. L. H., Yucel, G. H., Cleary, K. M., & Donkers, F. C. L. (2011). The neural circuitry of autism. *Neurotoxicity Research, 20*(3), 201–214. doi:10.1007/s12640-010-9234-7

Belmonte, M. K., Allen, G., Beckel-Mitchener, A., Boulanger, L. M., Carper, R. A., & Webb, S. J. (2004). Autism and abnormal development of brain connectivity. *Journal of Neuroscience, 24*(42), 9228–9231. doi:10.1523/JNEUROSCI.3340-04.2004

Bolton, P., Macdonald, H., Pickles, A., Rios, P., Goode, S., Crowson, M., ... Rutter, M. (1994). A case-control family history study of autism. *Journal of Child Psychology and Psychiatry, 35*(5), 877–900. doi:10.1111/j.1469-7610.1994.tb02300.x

Christensen, L., Hutman, T., Rozga, A., Young, G. S., Ozonoff, S., Rogers, S. J., ... Sigman, M. (2010). Play and developmental outcomes in infant siblings of children with autism. *Journal of Autism and Developmental Disorders, 40*, 946–957. doi:10.1007/s10803-010-0941-y

Comi, A. M., Zimmerman, A. W., Frye, V. H., Law, P. A., & Peeden, J. N. (1999). Familial clustering of autoimmune disorders and evaluation of medical risk factors in autism. *Journal of Child Neurology, 14*(6), 388–394. doi:10.1177/088307389901400608

Croen, L. A., Grether, J. K., Yoshida, C. K., Odouli, R., & Van de Water, J. (2005). Maternal autoimmune diseases, asthma and allergies, and childhood autism spectrum disorders: A case-control study. *Archives of Pediatric and Adolescent Medicine, 159*(2), 151–157. doi:10.1001/archpedi.159.2.151

Dadds, M. R., Hunter, K., Hawes, D. J., Frost, A. D. J., Vassallo, S., Bunn, P., ... Masry, Y. E. (2008). A measure of affective and cognitive empathy in children using parent ratings. *Child Psychiatry and Human Development, 39*(2), 111–122. doi:10.1007/s10578-007-0075-4

Dalton, K. M., Nacewicz, B. M., Alexander, A. L., & Davidson, R. J. (2007). Gaze-fixation, brain activation, and amygdala volume in unaffected siblings of individuals with autism. *Biological Psychiatry, 61*, 512–520. doi:10.1016/j.biopsych.2006.05.019

Dawson, G., Webb, S., Schellenberg, G. D., Dager, S., Friedman, S., Aylward, E., & Richards, T. (2002). Defining the broader phenotype of autism: Genetic, brain, and behavioral perspectives. *Development and Psychopathology, 14*(3), 581–611. doi:10.1017.S0954579402003103

Eriksson, M. A., Westerlund, J., Anderlid, B. M., Gillberg, C., & Fernell, E. (2012). First-degree relatives of young children with autism spectrum disorders: Some gender aspects. *Research in Developmental Disabilities, 33*(5), 1642–1648. doi:10.1016/j.ridd.2012.03.025

Fidler, D. J., Bailey, J. N., & Smalley, S. L. (2000). Macrocephaly in autism and other pervasive developmental disorders. *Developmental Medicine and Child Neurology, 42*(11), 737–740. doi:10.1111/j.1469-8749.2000.tb00035.x

Floris, D. L., Chura, L. R., Holt, R. J., Suckling, J., Bullmore, E. T., Baron-Cohen, S., & Spencer, M. D. (2013). Psychological correlates of handedness and corpus callosum asymmetry in autism: The left hemisphere dysfunction theory revisited. *Journal of Autism and Developmental Disorders, 43*(8), 1758–1772. doi:10.1007/s10803-012-1720-8

Gerdts, J., & Bernier, R. (2011). The broader autism phenotype and its implications on the etiology and treatment of autism spectrum disorders. *Autism Research and Treatment, 2011*, 1–19. (Open access article). Article ID 545901. doi:10.1155/2011/545901

Goussé, V., Plumet, M.-H., Chabane, N., Mouren-Simeoni, M.-C., Ferradian, N., & Leboyer, M. (2002). Fringe phenotypes in autism: A review of clinical, biochemical, and cognitive studies. *European Psychiatry, 17*(3), 120–128. doi:10.1016/S0924-9338(02)00640-5

Greimel, E., Schulte-Ruther, M., Kircher, T., Kamp-Becker, I., Remschmidt, H., Fink, G. R., ... Konrad, K. (2010). Neural mechanisms of empathy in adolescents with autism spectrum disorder and their fathers. *NeuroImage, 49*(1), 1055–1065. doi:10.1016/j.neuroimage.2009.07.057

Herbert, M. R. (2005). Large brains in autism: The challenge of pervasive abnormality. *The Neuroscientist, 11*(5), 417–440. doi:10.1177/0091270005278866

Holmboe, K., Elsabbagh, M., Volein, A., Tucker, L. A., Baron-Cohen, S., Bolton, P., ... Johnson, M. H. (2010). Frontal cortex functioning in the infant broader autism phenotype. *Infant Behavior and Development, 33*(4), 482–491. doi:10.1016/j.infbeh.2010.05.004

Hurley, R. S. E., Losh, M., Parlier, M., Reznick, J. S., & Piven, J. (2007). The broad autism phenotype questionnaire. *Journal of Autism and Developmental Disorders, 37*(9), 1679–1690. doi:10.1007/s10803-006-0299-3

Ingudomnukul, E., Baron-Cohen, S., Wheelwright, S., & Knickmeyer, R. (2007). Elevated rates of testosterone-related disorders in women with autism spectrum conditions. *Hormones and Behavior, 51*(5), 597–604. doi:10.1016/j.yhbeh.2007.02.001

Keil, A., Daniels, J. L., Forssen, U., Hultman, C., Cnattingius, S., Soderberg, K. C., ... Sparen, P. (2010). Parental autoimmune diseases associated with autism spectrum disorders in offspring. *Epidemiology, 21*(6), 805–808. doi:10.1097/EDE.0b013e3181f26e3f

Lainhart, J. E., & Lange, N. (2011). The biological broader autism phenotype. In D. G. Amaral, G. Dawson, & D. H. Geschwind (Eds.), *Autism spectrum disorders* (pp. 477–509). New York, NY: Oxford University Press, Inc.

Lainhart, J. E., Ozonoff, S., Coon, H., Krasny, L., Dinh, E., Nice, J., & McMahon, W. (2002). Autism, regression, and the broader autism phenotype. *American Journal of Medical Genetics, 113*(3), 231–237. doi:10.1002/ajmg.10615

Lloyd-Fox, S., Blasi, A., Elwell, C. E., Charman, T., Murphy, D., & Johnson, M. H. (2013). Reduced neural sensitivity to social stimuli in infants at risk for autism. *Proceedings of the Royal Society B, 280*, 20123026. doi:10.1098/rspb.2012.3026

Lundstrom, S., Haworth, C. M. A., Carlstrom, E., Gillberg, C., Mill, J., Rastam, M., ... Reichenberg, A. (2010). Trajectories leading to autism spectrum disorders are affected by paternal age: Findings from two nationally representative twin studies. *Journal of Child Psychology and Psychiatry, 51*(7), 850–856. doi:10.1111/j.1469-7610.2010.02223.x

Mandy, W., Charman, T., Puura, K., & Skuse, D. H. (2014). Investigating the cross-cultural validity of *DSM-5* autism spectrum disorder: Evidence from Finnish and UK samples. *Autism, 18*(1), 45–54. doi:10.1177/1362361313508026

Mehrabian, A. (1997). Relations among personality scales of aggression, violence, and empathy: Validational evidence bearing on the risk of eruptive violence scale. *Aggressive Behavior, 23*(6), 433–445. doi:10.1002/(SICI)1098-2337(1997)23:6<433::AID-AB3>3.0.CO;2-H

Merriam-Webster, Inc. (2014). *Atopy*. Retrieved from http://www.merriam-webster.com/dictionary/atopy

Micali, N., Chakrabarti, S., & Fombonne, E. (2004). The broad autism phenotype: Findings from an epidemiological survey. *Autism, 8*(1), 21–37. doi:10.1177/1362361304040636

Miles, J. H., Hadden, L. L., Takahashi, T. N., & Hillman, R. E. (2000). Head circumference is an independent clinical finding associated with autism. *American Journal of Medical Genetics, 95*(4), 339–350. doi:10.1002/1096-8628(20001211)

Mills, J. D., Kavanagh, T., Kim, W. S., Chen, B. J., Kawahara, Y., Halliday, G. M., & Janitz, M. (2013). Unique transcriptome patterns of the white and grey matter corroborate structural and functional heterogeneity in the human frontal lobe. *PLoS One, 8*(10), e78480. doi:10.1371/journal.pone.0078480

Mouridsen, S. E., Rich, B., Isager, T., & Nedergaard, N. J. (2007). Autoimmune diseases in parents of children with infantile autism: A case-control study. *Developmental Medicine & Child Neurology, 49*(6), 429–432. doi:10.1111/j.1469-8749.2007.00429.x

Newshaffer, C. J., Croen, L. A., Fallin, M. D., Hertz-Picciotto, I., Nguyen, D. V., Lee, N. L., ... Shedd-Wise, K. M. (2012). Infant siblings and the investigation of autism risk factors. *Journal of Neurodevelopmental Disorders, 4*(1), 7. (Open access article). doi:10.1186/1866-1955-4-7

Pelphrey, K., Adolphs, R., & Morris, J. P. (2004). Neuroanatomical substrates of social cognition dysfunction in autism. *Mental Retardation and Developmental Disabilities Research Reviews, 10*(4), 259–271. doi:10.1002/mrdd.20040

Puleo, C. M., Reichenberg, A., Smith, C. J., Kryzak, L. A., & Silverman, J. M. (2008). Do autism-related personality traits explain higher paternal age in autism? *Molecular Psychiatry, 13*(3), 243–244. doi:10.1038/sj.mp.4002102

Randolph-Gips, M., & Srinivasan, P. (2012). Modeling autism: A systems biology approach. *Journal of Clinical Bioinformatics, 2*, 17. (Open access article). Retrieved from http://www.jclinbioinformatics.com/content/2/1/17

Rojas, D. C., Teale, P. D., Majarajh, K., Kronberg, E., Youngpeter, K., Wilson, L. B., ... Hepburn, S. (2011). Transient and steady-state auditory gamma-band responses in first-degree relatives of people with autism spectrum disorder. *Molecular Autism, 2*, 11–23. doi:10.1186/2040-2392-2-11

Rutter, M. L. (2011). Progress in understanding autism: 2007–2010. *Journal of Autism and Developmental Disorders, 41*(4), 395–404. doi:10.1007/s10803-011-1184-2

Saresella, M., Marventano, I., Guerini, F. R., Mancuso, R., Ceresa, L., Zanzottera, M., ... Clerici, M. (2009). An autistic endophenotype results in complex immune dysfunction in healthy siblings of autistic children. *Biological Psychiatry, 66*(10), 978–984. doi:10.1016/j.biopsych.2009.06.020

Sweeten, T. L., Bowyer, S. L., Posey, D. J., Halberstadt, G. M., & McDougle, C. J. (2003). Increased prevalence of familial autoimmunity in probands with pervasive developmental disorders. *Pediatrics, 112*(5), e420–e424.

Valicenti-McDermott, M., McVicar, K., Rapin, I., Wershil, B. K., Cohen, H., & Shinnar, S. (2006). Frequency of gastrointestinal symptoms in children with autistic spectrum disorders and association with family history of autoimmune disease. *Journal of Developmental and Behavioral Pediatrics, 27*(2), S128–S136.

Vladeanu, M., Monteith-Hodge, E. M., & Bourne, V. J. (2012). Strength of lateralization for processing facial emotion in relation to autistic traits in individuals without autism. *Laterality: Asymmetries of Body, Brain and Cognition, 17*(4), 438–452. doi:10.1080/1357650X.2010.513385

Witkin, H. A., Dyk, R. B., Faterson, H. F., Goodenough, D. G., & Karp, S. A. (1962). *Personality through perception.* New York, NY: Harper and Row.

Zwaigenbaum, L., Szatmari, P., Jones, M. B., Bryson, S. E., Maclean, J. E., Mahoney, W. J., ... Tuff, L. (2002). Pregnancy and birth complications in autism and liability to the broader autism phenotype. *Journal of the American Academy of Child and Adolescent Psychiatry, 41*(5), 572–579. doi:10.1097/00004583-200205000-00015

CHAPTER 5

COGNITIVE FUNCTIONING IN THE BROAD AUTISM PHENOTYPE

Various types of cognitive functioning have been explored among people with autism spectrum disorder (ASD). These include cognitive abilities that traditionally have interested psychologists, such as attention (Reiersen & Todd, 2008), intelligence (Dykens & Lense, 2011), and executive functions (Happé, Booth, Charlton, & Hughes, 2006). Researchers also have studied areas of cognitive functioning that pertain more specifically to ASD, such as central coherence (Happé, 2005), theory of mind (Wahlberg, 2001), and social cognition (Gallese, 2006). In like manner, scientists have examined these same aspects of cognitive functioning in individuals who have or are believed to have the broad autism phenotype (BAP). This chapter discusses the findings of recent investigations concerning cognitive functioning in relation to the BAP.

5.1. PERCEPTION AND VISUAL ATTENTION

During the past decade, scientists have conducted studies involving parents and siblings of people with ASD to learn about their abilities in the areas of cognitive processing and attention. One of these (De la Marche, Steyaert, & Noens, 2012) examined the issue of atypical sensory perception. Many people on the autism spectrum manifest unusual sensory experiences such as extreme sensitivity to lights or sounds (Grandin, 2011). Therefore, De la Marche and colleagues (2012) reasoned that non-affected adolescents whose siblings have ASD also might demonstrate sensory processing that is out of the ordinary. They recruited teenagers with ASD and teenaged siblings of people with ASD, as well as typically developing teens to serve as a control group. Members of the sibling group were checked for the presence of undiagnosed ASD using the Social Responsiveness Scale (SRS; Constantino & Gruber, 2005). Six siblings whose SRS scores exceeded the cutoff score were removed from the study. The remaining participants included adolescents with ASD, siblings, and neurotypical controls.

To assess the nature of the participants' sensory processing experiences, De la Marche et al. (2012) administered a Dutch version of a 60-item self-report instrument called the Adolescent/Adult Sensory Profile (AASP; Brown & Dunn, 2002). This measure derives from a model of sensory processing that is based on two dimensions: "high vs low neurological threshold and active vs passive reaction" (De la Marche et al., 2012, p. 640). The AASP yields scores for four different types of sensory profiles, depending on an individual's sensory threshold in combination with his or her reaction to a particular sensory experience (De la Marche et al., 2012). As the authors discovered, participants in the sibling group obtained scores for the sensation seeking profile that were significantly higher than in the ASD group yet significantly lower than sensation seeking scores in the control group. The sensation seeking profile represents the combination of a high sensory threshold and an active reaction to sensations. Because siblings of people with ASD reported significantly lower sensation seeking than what was found among the control group, De la Marche and associates (2012) stated that the siblings also exhibit atypical sensory processing. The researchers further proposed that lower sensation seeking might represent an "intermediate phenotype" (De la Marche et al., 2012, p. 639) between full-blown ASD and typical neurological development. Although these authors did not use the label of BAP to describe this so-called intermediate phenotype, it is possible that individuals who meet criteria for the BAP have atypical sensory processing.

Another type of cognitive processing, action perception, served as the focus of an investigation by Ahmed and Vander Wyk (2013). They chose to study unaffected siblings of children with ASD, to learn whether such siblings show increased activation in the posterior superior temporal sulcus (pSTS) of the brain when viewing intentional actions. This area of the brain "is involved in extracting social meaning (intention) from bodily action" (Ahmed & Vander Wyk, 2013, p. 298). Three groups of youngsters participated in this study: children diagnosed with ASD, children who were unaffected siblings of individuals with ASD, and neurotypical children. There were no significant differences in age among the three groups; also, the compositions of the sibling group and control group were matched in terms of gender.

All participants underwent functional magnetic resonance imaging (fMRI) while watching a brief film. The film depicted an actor seated behind a table, with a blue cup and a white cup positioned side by side on the far side of the tabletop. The actor displayed either positive or negative emotion (i.e., either a smile or a frown) toward the blue cup on a table. Next, the actor chose either one cup or the other and moved it to the center of the table nearest the actor, while showing a neutral facial expression. Ahmed and Vander Wyk (2013) were interested in how the participants' brains would respond to emotionally congruent or incongruent actions made by the person in the film. Congruent actions consisted either of moving the blue cup after smiling at it, or moving the white cup after frowning at the blue cup. Incongruent actions involved either moving the white cup after smiling at the blue cup, or moving the blue cup after frowning at it.

Previous research had revealed that in contrast to children with ASD, neurotypical children showed greater activation of the pSTS in response to incongruent actions as compared to congruent actions. In this study, members of the control group did demonstrate significantly greater activation in this brain region when shown emotionally incongruent actions. However, fMRI results of the sibling group did not show heightened activation of the pSTS in response to viewing incongruent actions. Furthermore, the brain activation patterns of the sibling group more closely resembled those of children with ASD. Consequently, Ahmed and Vander Wyk (2013) suggested that an unusual pSTS response to incongruent purposeful actions is a feature shared by children with ASD and their siblings.

Visual attention abilities of individuals with the BAP have been explored in several studies. At least three of them have included infants who have a sibling with ASD. These babies are deemed to be at increased risk for ASD, and it is possible that some of them may eventually fit the definition of the BAP.

Rutherford (2013) performed a longitudinal study of infants who had ASD siblings and similarly aged infants with no ASD relatives, comparing these two groups on three visual attention tasks that contained a social element. Each participating infant was strapped into a car seat and its eye movements were monitored. In a face preference task, each baby viewed a series of 10 color photographs of a human face. A rectangular neutral image of the same size was simultaneously shown next to the face in each trial. This neutral image was derived from the photograph of the face used in that trial and looked like a mottled gray sheet of paper, which was matched to its corresponding face in terms of high, medium, and low visual frequency components. The two images were shown for 5 seconds, during which eye tracker equipment measured the amount of time that the infant looked at the facial image.

During an eyes preference task, each participating infant was shown a series of 10 different color photographs of human faces for 5 seconds per face. Within each trial, eye tracking equipment assessed whether the baby looked at either the eyes or the mouth portion of the face.

The third visual attention task in Rutherford's (2013) study was a so-called chase preference task. Each infant in the study participated in two 90-second trials involving two side-by-side computer monitors. One of the monitors displayed a socially relevant scenario depicting two dots moving on the screen as if one dot were chasing the other. The other monitor showed two dots moving at similar speeds but did not present any relationship between them. Data were recorded concerning the amount of time that the baby spent looking at each of the two monitors. The chase preference trials were videotaped and coded by expert raters, who achieved a high rate of inter-rater agreement.

Participants in Rutherford's (2013) study initially were measured at 3 months of age and were reevaluated when they were 6 months old. Findings revealed that the neurotypical infants exhibited a stronger preference for looking at social stimuli. Moreover, group differences between the control group and the siblings group increased over time. Infants in the control group demonstrated increasing interest in eyes and faces from ages 3 to 6 months, while the infants in the ASD sibling group showed no such change over that same time frame.

Another study of visual orienting, conducted by Elison et al. (2013), employed 7-month-old infants as participants. This large team of researchers obtained access to a sample of infants, roughly half of which had siblings with ASD. The other babies had no first- or second-degree relatives with ASD and showed no symptoms of ASD on a screening instrument called the Social Communication Questionnaire (SCQ; Berument, Rutter, Lord, Pickles, & Bailey, 1999). All of the infant participants were shown a series of complex visual stimuli that included 10 different objects and 10 different faces. Eye-tracking equipment was used to determine how long it took each participant to move his or her eyes away from a central visual image to a new image appearing on a screen.

When the infants were 25 months old, all of them underwent clinical assessment using the Autism Diagnostic Observation Schedule (ADOS; Lord et al., 2000). At that time, 16 infants in the sibling group received a diagnosis of ASD. The other members of the sibling group were classified as "high-risk negative" (Elison et al., 2013, p. 899), that is, they did not meet criteria for ASD. Results of this study found no significant differences between the high-risk negative siblings and the low-risk infants with regard to visual orienting latencies, although the siblings who did receive an ASD diagnosis showed longer orienting latencies in comparison to the other two groups of infants in this study.

Infants in the age range of 9–10 months who had siblings with ASD participated in a study of visual orienting performed by Elsabbagh and colleagues (2009). This team of scientists used a research paradigm known as "the Gap-overlap task, which measures differences in the efficiency of orienting towards peripheral stimuli" (Elsabbagh et al., 2009, p. 638). Infant siblings in this study were compared to an age- and gender-matched group of babies who had no first- or second-degree relatives with ASD. Each participant sat on a parent's lap before a computer monitor and was videotaped in a series of visual trials. During such a trial, the infant participant was shown an animated central image, after which an image of a moving green balloon appeared either to the right or left of center and at an angle to central image. This peripheral image stayed on the screen until the baby looked at it, or until 3 seconds had gone by.

Elsabbagh et al. (2009) created three different conditions for their study. A baseline condition consisted of removing the central image at the same time that the peripheral image was shown. A gap condition involved removing the central image 200 ms before presenting the peripheral image. An overlap condition involved continued presentation of the central image after the peripheral image appeared, such that both images appeared on the screen. However, in the overlap condition, the central image was no longer in motion once the peripheral target appeared on the viewing screen. Participants were shown these three conditions in random order during two blocks that consisted of 35 trials apiece, continuing until such time that the baby became fussy or until 70 trials were presented.

Based on the visual reaction times of the infants in their study, Elsabbagh and associates (2009) examined two types of dependent variables: a disengagement effect and a facilitation effect. The disengagement measure told the researchers how efficiently the infants shifted their gaze from the central to the peripheral image, while the facilitation measure pertained to the speed of visual orienting when a gap preceded the presentation of the peripheral stimulus. Elsabbagh et al. (2009) found that in comparison to the controls, infant siblings took longer to disengage from the central stimulus. Additionally, members of the sibling group showed less facilitation when a time delay preceded the introduction of the peripheral visual stimulus. Thus, Elsabbagh et al. (2009) concluded that at-risk infant siblings of people with ASD have an atypical pattern of visual orienting that may be associated with the BAP. These authors hypothesized that their findings might have clinical relevance. Nevertheless, they also recognized that early indications of unusual visual orienting might be insufficient as a risk marker, and might need to be used in combination with other factors to predict whether or not an infant might eventually warrant a diagnosis of ASD.

Older siblings of children with ASD also have been included in studies of visual attention. For example, Belmonte, Gomot, and Baron-Cohen (2010) recruited 11- to 15-year-old males to investigate differences in complex visual processing. Three groups of youths participated in this study: persons with ASD, siblings of individuals with ASD, and typically developing young men. Only one person in the sibling group was related to a member of the ASD group. All participants were of at least average intellectual functioning, and the three groups were comparable in terms of both verbal and nonverbal intelligence.

The participants completed two runs of visual trials, with each run consisting of 166 stimulus arrays that were shown for 3 seconds per trial. Each trial presented a nonsocial, divided attention task involving two side-by-side, complex visual arrays that varied according to the color, position, and orientation (i.e., angled upward or downward) of objects in each image. Participants needed to attend to a central object in each of the two arrays, and were instructed to press a button to indicate when the screen showed the proper color of the central object on one side and proper orientation of the central object on the other side. As indicated by the results of this study, the unaffected siblings group performed more accurately than the ASD group but less accurately than the neurotypical control group. Belmonte et al. (2010) stated that the results of the ASD group and the sibling group were qualitatively similar, and suggested that these similarities were due to abnormalities in activation of the frontal cortex among these participants.

Parents of children with ASD comprise another group whose visual attention abilities have been studied. Scheeren and Stauder (2008) recruited parents of children with ASD and compared them to parents of neurotypical children. Both groups of parents were similar in terms of gender composition, age, educational level, and performance on a measure of central coherence. Also, there were no significant differences between groups with regard to their scores on the Autism-Spectrum Quotient (AQ; Baron-Cohen, Wheelwright, Skinner, Martin, & Clubley, 2001), which measures traits associated with ASD.

In Scheeren and Stauder's (2008) study, visual attention was examined through reaction-time tasks involving two kinds of visual cues. The experimental task required participants to press a button when an A appeared on a computer screen, but to refrain from pressing the button when an X appeared on the screen. Either a social or a nonsocial cue preceded the appearance of the target letter, to indicate whether the target would appear on either the left or right side of the computer screen.

During the social or eye task condition, the visual trial began by showing a female face in the center of the computer screen. The woman's eyes initially looked straight ahead for 500 ms, but then looked either to the left or to the right for 400 ms. When the target letter appeared onscreen, the face at the center of the screen disappeared. In the nonsocial or arrow task condition, a set of arrows were shown in the center of the computer screen, with one arrow pointing left and the other arrow pointing right for 500 ms. Next, both arrows would point either to the right or left side of the screen for 400 ms, followed by the presentation of the target letter on the screen. An equal number of congruent and incongruent trials were included in each of two sets of 60 trials. In a congruent trial, the eyes or arrow pointed to the side of the computer screen where the target letter would appear; during an incongruent trial, the eyes or arrows would point to the side of the computer that was opposite the side where the target was presented.

Scheeren and Stauder's (2008) study found that fathers of children with ASD were significantly slower on the eye task as compared to the arrow task. According to the researchers, this result signified that the fathers of ASD children have difficulty processing information communicated by another person's eyes. Also, in comparison to fathers of typically developing children, fathers of children with ASD were significantly slower in reaction time. However, there were no significant differences between the two groups of mothers with regard to reaction time. This gender-based performance disparity prompted Scheeren and Stauder (2008) to speculate that fathers of children with ASD may have more noticeable BAP characteristics than mothers of these children.

Because ASD traits have been found even in the general population (Lai, Lombardo, Chakrabarti, & Baron-Cohen, 2013), Bayliss and Kritikos (2011) performed a study of visual attention in a sample of individuals with a high number of ASD characteristics. This study may shed light on the BAP since the distinction between someone with the BAP and someone who has a large number of ASD features currently is arbitrary (Mandy, Charman, Puura, & Skuse, 2014). Furthermore, individuals with the BAP are present in the populace at large.

The research question posed by Bayliss and Kritikos (2011) concerned whether sensitivity to visual load differs according to someone's position on the autism spectrum in a general population. To investigate this issue, the scientists used a method known as a flanker task. Each participant in their study looked at a computer monitor that displayed a cross in the center of the screen, surrounded by either two or four letters that appeared at the points of an imaginary square around the central cross. In the two-letter condition, small dots were presented on the screen in the corners of the square that were without letters. The letters H, K, V, Y, and Z served as distractor letters, while the target letters for this task were N and X. In addition to either two or four letters surrounding the central cross, a larger letter appeared to the side of the letters that formed the imaginary square (In other words, the larger letter was the flanker.) Participants were told to look at the central cross on the screen, ignore the large flanking letter, look for either the letter N or the letter X in the area surrounding the cross, and press the corresponding letter key on the computer keyboard.

Besides varying the perceptual load through random presentations of either two- and four-letter conditions, Bayliss and Kritikos (2011) included another variable that they called compatibility. This variable had two possible conditions: neutral and incompatible. In the neutral condition, the flanker was not one of the target letters. In the incompatible condition, one of the target letters appeared surrounding the circle while the other target letter served as the flanker.

Participants in the Bayliss and Kritikos (2011) study consisted of undergraduate students who completed not only the flanker task but also the AQ (mentioned earlier in this chapter). Those whose AQ score equaled or exceeded 15 were categorized as the high AQ group; all others were classified as the low AQ group. Although there were several fewer members in the high AQ group, the two groups were generally comparable in terms of group size, age, and gender composition. Results of this investigation showed no between-group differences in terms of accuracy or reaction time. Also, the two groups performed similarly on the two-letter condition. However, members of the high AQ group experienced more interference on the flanker task when the perceptual load was increased to the four-letter set. Based on a comparison of their results to the findings of prior research, Bayliss and Kritikos (2011) wrote that "the high AQ group might be indistinguishable from a sample of people with autism" (p. 1577). Their results are particularly interesting because their high AQ group contained almost three times as many females as males. However, because the same gender ratio existed in the low AQ group, these authors argued that AQ score was more important than gender in influencing individual differences in attention ability.

In summary, findings of studies that have examined perception and visual attention suggest that individuals with the BAP attend less to social stimuli and experience difficulty in extracting information from social stimuli. They also may have trouble paying attention to complex visual stimuli and may demonstrate greater interference in reaction time as the visual perceptual load increases. Additionally, although results of the studies described here are equivocal, it appears likely that people with the BAP take more time than neurotypical individuals to orient to visual stimuli.

5.2. FACE PROCESSING

A few of the aforementioned studies examined visual attention to social stimuli. Others have focused specifically on the ability of persons with the BAP to process faces. Siblings of individuals with ASD, parents of children with ASD, and neurotypical adults with ASD traits have participated in these investigations.

Young children who had siblings with ASD took part in a study of face-processing ability that was performed by de Klerk, Gliga, Charman, Johnson, and the BASIS team (2014). This group of colleagues knew from earlier research that infants at risk for ASD still orient to human faces, but they also were aware that children with ASD have trouble with face recognition. Therefore, de Klerk et al. (2014) wanted to learn whether siblings of children with ASD might have similar difficulty in recognizing faces. Participants in their study formed two groups. The high-risk group contained youngsters who were 3 years of age and had an older sibling with ASD; the low-risk group consisted of children of similar age who had a neurotypical older sibling. There was a statistically significant difference between groups in the area of general intelligence. The mean intelligence quotient (IQ) of the low-risk group fell into the high-average range whereas the mean IQ of the high-risk group was in the average range. Otherwise, both groups were comparable with regard to gender composition, fine motor ability, visual ability, and receptive and expressive language.

Each child sat in a caregiver's lap during the administration of a face recognition task. The child looked at a computer screen that showed a picture of a human face wearing a neutral expression. This image was presented for 5,000 ms, after which it was replaced for 3,000 ms by an image of a house with two empty windows. The experimenter told the child that the person whose face had been shown had gone into the house. Next, the house displayed two faces, one in each window. One of the faces was the same as that which had been shown earlier, while the other was a new face. The experimenter asked the child to touch the face of the person who had been seen previously. The image showing two faces remained on the computer screen until the child responded or until 7,000 ms had elapsed.

Twelve face recognition trials were presented at two levels of difficulty. Six of the trials were easy, involving the use of the identical photo that had been shown during the initial presentation of the target face. During the six difficult trials, the facial expression of the target face changed from the original expression (either neutral expression or a close-mouthed smile) to another expression such as an open-mouthed smile.

Data in the study by de Klerk et al. (2014) yielded a significant difference between the two groups. The low-risk group recognized faces at better than chance levels for both the easy and difficult recognition tasks. The high-risk group performed better than chance for the easy task but performed only at the level of chance on the difficult task. The authors of this inquiry pointed out that the obtained group differences in performance could not be attributed to an ASD diagnosis or to ASD-like communication problems. Also, group differences in face recognition ability held true even after controlling for group differences in IQ. Thus, de Klerk et al. (2014) concluded that "face-processing difficulties are an endophenotype of ASD that is present in those at familial risk" (p. 604).

Because not only siblings but also parents of children with ASD may meet criteria for the BAP, a 2010 study by Wallace, Sebastian, Pellicano, Parr, and Bailey recruited both of these high-risk groups for a face-processing study. Their participants included three approximately equal groups: neurotypical adult controls, people with ASD, and parents and adult siblings of ASD-diagnosed individuals from multiple-incidence ASD families. The latter group was referred to as the relatives group; no members of this group were related to each other or to the participants in the ASD group. All three groups were similar with regard to participants' age, receptive vocabulary level, and nonverbal problem-solving ability as measured by Ravens Standard Progressive Matrices (Raven, Court, & Raven, 1992).

Participants engaged in three kinds of face-processing tasks, all of which were administered via laptop computer. First, they were asked to distinguish between unfamiliar faces. The second task examined participants' ability to recognize facial expressions of happiness, sadness, fear, anger, surprise, and disgust as well as a neutral facial expression, when they were shown faces that were either upright or upside-down. The third task required them to identify directional cues that were given by either a pair of eyes shown within a face, or only the eyes portion of a face, or a pair of arrows (Wallace et al., 2010).

Although the relatives group performed better than the ASD group on the face discrimination task, they were less capable than neurotypical adults at differentiating faces. The relatives group also did significantly worse than the neurotypical control participants at recognizing facial expressions of disgust or fear. Additionally, and in contrast to the typically developed adults in this study, neither the relatives group nor the ASD group demonstrated sensitivity to the direct eye gaze condition during the directional cues task. Wallace et al. (2010) concluded that at least some relatives of persons with ASD display unusual patterns of face processing, and hypothesized that such abnormalities potentially could serve as a cognitive endophenotype for ASD.

Parents of children with ASD served as participants in several additional studies of face-processing ability. Palermo, Pasqualetti, Barbati, Intelligente, and Rossini (2006) compared parents of children with ASD to matched controls on a task that involved drawings of men's faces which depicted five basic facial expressions: happiness, sadness, surprise, anger, and disgust. The researchers chose these five emotions because they wished to focus on emotional expressions that people routinely encounter in daily life. Participants were asked to identify which of the five emotions was being shown in each facial drawing. Palermo et al. (2006) learned that fathers of children with ASD had more trouble than mothers of children with ASD in correctly recognizing facial expressions of disgust or sadness. However, both fathers and mothers of children with ASD were less successful than control participants in this regard.

When Adolphs, Spezio, Parlier, and Piven (2008) conducted their study of face-processing ability in parents of children with ASD, they assessed the parents for the presence of the BAP using the Modified Personality Assessment Schedule-Revised (i.e., M-PAS-R; Piven et al., 1997). Parents were classified according to whether or not they met M-PAS-R criteria for aloofness. Thus, the participants in the Adolphs et al. (2008) study comprised three groups. Some parents of children with ASD were categorized as BAP+ because they exhibited social aloofness. The BAP− group consisted of non-aloof parents of children with ASD, and the control group contained parents of typically developing children. These three groups of adults were comparable in terms of age, intellectual functioning, race, socioeconomic status, level of educational attainment, and visual ability. Participants were asked to identify the emotions of either happiness or fear when shown facial photographs in which only a portion of the eyes and mouth could be seen. In comparison to the control participants, those in the BAP+ group were far less likely to look at the eyes and far more likely to look at the mouths in the photographs. Results of the BAP− group fell in the range between the results of the other two groups. Adolphs and colleagues (2008) noted that the face-processing patterns of their BAP+ group were remarkably similar to the face-processing patterns of people with ASD.

Wilson, Freeman, Brock, Burton, and Palermo (2010) used a different instrument, the Broad Autism Phenotype Questionnaire (BAPQ; Hurley, Losh, Parlier, Reznick, & Piven, 2007), to determine whether parents of children with ASD possessed characteristics of the BAP. They performed two experiments involving the facial recognition abilities of parents who had children with ASD. In the first experiment, parents completed the Cambridge Face Memory Test (CFMT; Duchaine & Nakayama, 2006), a computer-administered instrument designed to measure a person's ability to learn and recognize new faces. During the second experiment, parents and their children completed a computerized task that involved not only recognizing photographs of faces but also photographs of shoes. The purpose of the second experiment was to examine the relationship between parents' and children's facial recognition abilities. Wilson et al. (2010) were curious about this topic because a few studies (e.g., Wilmer et al., 2010; Zhu et al., 2010) have reported that facial recognition skill is heritable.

Results of the Wilson et al. (2010) investigation were equivocal. On the one hand, the first experiment indicated that the parents in this study performed significantly below average on the CFMT. In particular, the fathers in this study demonstrated impairment on this test. However, the scientists found no relationship between parents' scores on the BAPQ and performance on the CFMT. Additionally, parents exhibited no impairment on a simple face recognition task that they completed during the second experiment, even though their children with ASD did reveal impaired performance. The authors of this research concluded that aspects of facial recognition ability may be deficient in some relatives of people with ASD. However, they cautioned that due to the heterogeneity of ASD symptoms, future researchers should not assume that consistent behavioral patterns will be apparent in the relatives of individuals with ASD.

More recently, Kadak, Demirel, Yavuz, and Demir (2014) employed the AQ (Baron-Cohen, Wheelwright, Skinner, et al., 2001) to check for the presence of the BAP among parents who took part in their study about facial expressions of emotion. This team of investigators conducted their study in Turkey, recruiting parents of children with ASD and parents of typically developing youngsters. All of the parents completed the AQ as well as the Emotion Recognition Test, which the researchers devised on the basis of photographs assembled by Ekman and Friesen (1976). This computer-administered test consisted of 56 photographs that included both men and women displaying facial expressions of happiness, sadness, fear, anger, disgust, and surprise, as well as a neutral expression. An equal number of pictures for each emotion were shown in random order to each participant. The data from this study revealed that parents of children with ASD showed significantly greater deficits in social skills as measured by the AQ. When compared to parents of typically developing children, the parents of children with ASD also had significantly greater trouble in correctly identifying neutral and surprised faces. Kadak et al. (2014) surmised that similar to children with ASD, their parents also have problems with recognizing neutral facial expressions.

Neurotypical adults with a high level of ASD traits also have been studied in regard to face-processing ability. For example, Miu, Pana, and Avram (2012) screened students attending a university in Romania by administering the AQ. From an initial pool of 295 individuals, 81 students were selected on the basis of their AQ score. Thirty women and four men comprised a group that was deemed high in autistic traits (AT) because their scores on the AQ exceeded one standard deviation above the mean of the beginning sample. The low AT group, containing 39 women and 8 men, obtained AQ scores that were one standard deviation below the mean of the initial large group. Both groups of participants underwent observational fear conditioning as well as a test of visual attention bias, and they completed a Romanian version of the Reading the Mind in the Eyes Test (RMET; Baron-Cohen, Wheelwright, Hill, Raste, & Plumb, 2001).

Fear conditioning was achieved by showing a brief movie that depicted a model receiving electrical shocks administered to the model's wrist when a colored square appeared on a computer screen. Participants were told that they were going to undergo the same test as the model in the movie. Although they never actually received electrical shocks, their skin conductance response was monitored as they partook in the same test that was shown in the movie.

The test of visual attention bias involved 384 trials, each of which began with participants looking at a fixation point on the center of a computer screen. Next, they were shown either a fearful face or a neutral face, followed by a target letter (upper-case T or L) that appeared to either the right or the left of the central point on the computer screen. Participants were asked to push a button on the computer, as quickly as possible, whenever one of the two target letters appeared.

In addition, participants in the study by Miu and colleagues (2012) were given a computer-administered version of the RMET. This test included 36 photographs showing only the eyes of a face, accompanied by four possible choices describing the emotional state of the person presented in each photograph. Participants were instructed to quickly choose which of the four words best described the photograph.

On the basis of these procedures, Miu et al. (2012) learned that the participants in the high AT group showed increased social learning of fear in the observational conditioning task, although they did not demonstrate a visual attention bias toward fearful faces. Additionally, the high AT group was comparable in accuracy to the low AT group on the RMET, but high AT participants took more time when responding to the items on this test. According to Miu et al. (2012), their findings "extend the cognitive and emotional similarities between ASD and AT" (p. 493) and contribute to understanding about the characteristics of the BAP.

Researchers in Belgium also used the AQ in their study of face processing among individuals with a high number of ASD features. Poljac, Poljac, and Wagemans (2012) gave a Dutch version of the AQ to a convenience sample of 500 undergraduate psychology students; from among this sample, the top 5% and the bottom 5% were chosen for further inclusion in the study. The high AT group contained 21 students (13 women and 8 men) while the low AT group consisted of 18 students (12 women and 6 men). There were no significant age differences between the two groups, and none of these participants had a family history of psychological or developmental disorders.

Participants in the study by Poljac et al. (2012) completed two tests of face processing. The first was a shortened version of the Benton Facial Recognition Test (Benton, Sivan, Hamsher, Varney, & Spreen, 1994), which provided a measure of basic ability for accurate facial recognition. This test was administered in the form of a booklet, with each page showing a target face and an array of six faces beneath the target. From the six choices, participants had to identity which face matched each target face.

The second test was the Emotion Recognition Task (ERT; Montagne, Kessels, De Haan, & Perrett, 2007) which presented a series of video segments, each of which began with the presentation of a neutral facial expression. During each video, the intensity of the emotion being depicted was gradually increased in stages of 10%, using morphed computer-generated images. Both male and female faces were included within the test, as were six basic emotional states (i.e., happiness, sadness, fear, anger, surprise, and disgust). When taking the ERT, participants each completed a total of 216 trials. Initially they were shown videos that went from a neutral face to 20% of an emotion's intensity. Next, they saw videos that went from the neutral expression to 30% intensity, and so on until all emotions and all actors had been shown and until all videos had gone from neutral to 100% intensity. Videos were shown in a randomized fashion. During each trial, each participant was required to choose which of the six emotions had been presented.

The outcome of this research was that members of the high AT group were less accurate at identifying facial expressions of sadness, anger, and disgust. In addition, high AT participants needed to see more intense facial displays in order to recognize facial expressions of emotion. Poljac et al. (2012) determined that one's ability to recognize emotional expressions corresponds to the degree of ASD traits in an individual, and they noted that their findings shed light on emotion processing in people with the BAP.

Undergraduates in Australia served in a study of face recognition conducted by Rhodes, Jeffery, Taylor, and Ewing (2013). All participants in this study completed the CFMT, previously described, as well as the AQ. A subset of the initial sample also completed a face identity aftereffect task (Jeffery et al., 2011). This test is based on the finding that seeing one face results in an altered perception of a subsequent face. Previous research had shown that face identity aftereffects are diminished in children with ASD; thus, Rhodes et al. (2013) wanted to learn whether individuals with a high degree of ASD characteristics might demonstrate a similar pattern. As expected, men's scores on the social scale of the AQ were negatively correlated with facial identity coding, and men with high AQ scores had more trouble on the facial recognition test. Surprisingly, however, a different pattern emerged for women. A high amount of autistic traits in women was positively correlated with coding of facial identity and bore no relationship to ability for face recognition. Therefore, Rhodes et al. (2013) proposed that unusual face coding might be an endophenotype for ASD in men, but they also speculated that ASD endophenotypes for women might be different from those for men.

A review of the studies described in this section suggests that at least some individuals with the BAP have trouble with face recognition. People with a high number of ASD features may experience problems in recognizing a variety of basic facial expressions and may require a more intense facial display in order to correctly discern the emotion being shown. Furthermore, they might mistakenly impart an emotional meaning to a neutral facial expression. Also, there is a possibility that gender differences may exist among BAP individuals with regard to face-processing ability.

5.3. PHONOLOGICAL PROCESSING

Gerdts and Bernier (2011) defined phonological processing as "the manner in which written and spoken words are processed" (p. 12). These authors reported that such processing difficulties are heritable and often are observed among children with ASD.

Several teams of scientists have explored whether phonological processing problems are common among relatives of children with ASD but have reached varying conclusions. In an early investigation of this topic, Bishop, Maybery, Wong, Hill, and Hallmayer (2004) recruited children with ASD, neurotypical children, and the parents and siblings of both groups of children. All participants were given two measures of phonological processing. The first of these was a nonword repetition test, and the second test required participants to read aloud two passages of text containing nonsense words. All parents also completed the AQ to check for the presence of the BAP.

Children with ASD who participated in this inquiry performed markedly worse than typically developing children on both of the phonological processing tests. However, the phonological processing of parents whose children had ASD was no different from that of parents of children in the control group. Parents whose AQ scores fell within the range of the BAP did report having a history of problems with language and reading, yet they did not obtain lower scores on either of the phonological tests. For this reason, Bishop and colleagues (2004) decided that impairment in phonological processing is not a component of the BAP.

Another group of researchers (Schmidt et al., 2008) compared parents of children with ASD to a matched group of parents of typically developing youngsters on a variety of cognitive and language tests. Parents of children with ASD showed no significant differences from parents of neurotypical children on tests of receptive language, expressive language, figurative language, and verbal fluency. They also were no more likely than control parents to have a history of reading difficulty, yet they did demonstrate problems on a test of nonword repetition. Thus, in contrast to Bishop et al. (2004), Schmidt et al. (2008) believed that phonological processing deficits are a possible element of the BAP.

In addition to nonword repetition and nonsense passage reading, rapid automatized naming (RAN) is another test of phonological processing ability. Losh, Esserman, and Piven (2010) incorporated this approach in their investigation of genetic markers for ASD. On the basis of previous research, Losh et al. (2010) knew that "RAN ability is highly heritable" (p. 110). They suspected that deficits in RAN might be a feature of the BAP and recruited parents of children with ASD to examine this possibility. Two different comparison groups also participated in this study: parents of children with Down syndrome, and parents of typically developing children. Parents were evaluated for the possible presence of the BAP via the M-PAS-R (Piven et al., 1997). They also completed portions of the Rapid Automatized Naming Task (Denckla & Rudel, 1974) that required them to quickly name randomly presented colors or objects that were presented in a series of rows. Results of this procedure revealed that parents of children with ASD took significantly longer to complete the RAN test. In addition, the social aspect of the BAP (as measured by the M-PAS-R) was associated with needing more time to finish the RAN task.

Based on their findings, Losh et al. (2010) reported that "BAP features among parents were associated with RAN performance" (p. 113). Nevertheless, they cautioned that their analyses were of an exploratory nature and needed to be replicated by further research.

Seeking to examine brain mechanisms that may underlie BAP-related language impairments, McFadden, Hepburn, Winterrowd, Schmidt, and Rojas (2012) recruited parents of children with ASD and a comparable number of adults who had no family history of developmental disorders. These participants underwent magnetoencephalography (MEG) while completing a test of word recognition, and they also completed a phonological test that involved repetition of nonwords. Results indicated that parents of children with ASD obtained significantly worse scores than controls on the phonological measure. Additionally, MEG revealed a different pattern of gamma-band brain waves for the two groups; parents of ASD children demonstrated an increase in evoked gamma-band activity while members of the control group manifested a decrease. McFadden and associates (2012) stated that theirs was the first study to explore gamma-band responses to language tasks in immediate relatives of individuals with ASD. They believed that further investigations of this type might yield a better understanding about the relationship between language ability and brain functioning in people with the BAP.

More recently, Wilson et al. (2013) claimed that deficient phonological processing is "a core BAP trait" (p. 1447). They explored this supposition by using an fMRI to scan the brains of parents of children with ASD and control participants. All participants in this study completed a nonword repetition test. Additionally, they engaged in a reading decision-making task while undergoing fMRI. They looked at visual stimuli on a screen and pressed a button to indicate whether each stimulus being presented was an actual word or a nonword. Results indicated that in relation to the comparison participants, parents of children with ASD demonstrated greater blood flow to brain regions that are involved in phonological processing during tasks that involved more phonological recoding. The fMRI data correlated with performance on the nonword repetition test and suggested that parents of children with ASD engaged in compensatory cognitive processing during phonological tasks. Consequently, Wilson and associates (2013) proposed that phonological processing differences in the brain appear to be a basic feature of the BAP. However, similar to Losh et al. (2012), Wilson et al. (2013) indicated that replication of their findings are necessary before any firm conclusions can be drawn.

5.4. LANGUAGE ABILITY

Deficits in language and communication ability have long been considered a part of the BAP. In 1997 Piven and colleagues utilized the Pragmatic Rating Scale (PRS; Landa et al., 1992) to evaluate the speech of parents whose children had ASD. These scientists reported that in comparison to the parents of children with Down syndrome, parents of ASD children exhibited more pragmatic language errors such as overly detailed, disorganized, or vague speech, unusual humor, or infrequent initiation of conversation. Parents of ASD children also exhibited unusual speech characteristics such as mispronunciations and abnormalities in volume, intonation, and rate of speech (Piven et al., 1997).

During their review of the BAP, Bailey, Palferman, Heavey, and Le Couteur (1998) also highlighted pragmatic language difficulties in the relatives of individuals diagnosed with ASD. They noted that up to that time, most studies about first-degree relatives of people with ASD reported language delays in at least some of the relatives. Bailey et al. (1998) also mentioned that problems with conversation and narrative speech were frequently observed among adults suspected of having the BAP.

Folstein et al. (1999) incorporated the PRS in a battery of tests that they administered to parents and siblings of 90 people with ASD, as well as parents and siblings of 40 individuals with Down syndrome. Siblings of ASD probands were not found to differ from siblings of Down syndrome probands with regard to a history of early language deficits; however, parents of ASD probands were more likely than parents of Down syndrome probands to have reported a history of language problems in childhood. Parents who complained of early language difficulties also obtained worse scores than control parents on the PRS. However, the presence or absence of early language deficits made no difference in terms of parents' performance on measures of social functioning such as the Friendship Interview (Santangelo & Folstein, 1995). Therefore, Folstein et al. (1999) speculated that language deficits comprise an aspect of the BAP that is genetically separate from its social aspect.

Several more recent studies also have examined language abilities in parents of children with ASD. Whitehouse, Barry, and Bishop (2007) sought to compare the language component of the BAP versus specific language impairment. Participants in their study consisted of three groups: parents of children with ASD, parents whose children had specific language impairment, and parents of neurotypical children. All of these parents completed a battery of standardized language assessments as well as the AQ. Interestingly, parents of children with ASD performed better than both other groups of parents on all of the language tests, yet they also manifested more difficulty with pragmatic language according to their scores on the AQ. Given these results, Whitehouse et al. (2007) concluded that the genetic etiology of ASD is distinct from the genetics that underlie the development of specific language impairment.

Losh, Childress, Lam, and Piven (2008) compared pragmatic language abilities of parents from simplex and multiplex ASD families, believing that this characteristic might be a possible marker for BAP genes. Their study included parents of children with Down syndrome as a comparison group and used the PRS to evaluate pragmatic language skills. According to their findings, parents from multiplex ASD families made more errors in speech and pragmatic language than parents from simplex ASD families, who in turn committed more such errors than the parents of children with Down syndrome.

The PRS again served as a measure of pragmatic language use in a 2012 study performed by Losh and colleagues. During this investigation, the researchers compared mothers of children with ASD to mothers of children with Fragile X syndrome as well as a control group comprised of mothers of neurotypical children. The mothers of children with ASD were found not to differ significantly from the mothers of children with Fragile X in terms of the number of pragmatic language errors that they made. However, both of these groups made more mistakes in pragmatic language than the control mothers.

Taylor et al. (2013) took a slightly different approach during their inquiry concerning the relationship between the BAP and communication deficits. This group of scientists looked at language abilities in children with ASD when one or both parents had the BAP, in comparison to ASD children whose parents did not have the BAP. BAP classification of parents was accomplished through the administration of the AQ. The language abilities of their children with ASD were evaluated by having the parents complete the second edition of the Children's Communication Checklist (CCC-2; Bishop, 2003). This instrument assesses structural aspects of language such as grammar and syntax, in addition to pragmatic language skills such as the inappropriate initiation of conversation and the use of context during communication. CCC-2 scores were significantly higher for children whose parents did not have the BAP, as compared to the other two groups of youngsters. The scores of children with one BAP parent were comparable to those who had two BAP parents, with the exception of scores on the social scale of the CCC-2. On that scale, ASD children who had two parents with the BAP scored significantly worse than children with ASD who had only one parent with the BAP (Taylor et al., 2013).

In their review of the literature regarding the BAP in parents of children with ASD, Cruz, Carmagos-Junior, and Rocha (2013) wrote that impairments in pragmatic language seem to be a component of the BAP. However, these authors also cautioned that this assumption has not yet been fully confirmed and requires additional investigation.

Siblings of children with ASD also have participated in studies examining language abilities of the BAP. Gamliel, Yirmiya, Jaffe, Manor, and Sigman (2009) conducted a longitudinal study in which they tracked siblings of children with ASD and compared them to siblings of neurotypical children. Language skills of the participants in this research were measured over a time interval spanning from 4 months to 7 years of age, using a variety of standardized instruments. By the time the siblings of ASD children reached age 7, 40% of them demonstrated not only language difficulties but also deficits in cognition and academic performance. This subgroup of participants was classified as having the BAP. A comparison of scores on language tests that were completed between 14 and 54 months of age revealed that both groups of siblings with ASD (i.e., regardless of BAP status) obtained language scores that were significantly lower than the scores of children who had typically developing siblings.

Along similar lines, Ben-Yizhak et al. (2011) obtained a group of school-aged children whose siblings had ASD and compared their language skills to those of school-aged children with neurotypical siblings. Children of ASD siblings were subdivided into BAP and non-BAP groups. Those in the BAP group were classified as such because they obtained an algorithm score of 4 or higher on the Autism Diagnostic Observation Scale (ADOS; Lord, Rutter, DiLavore, & Risi, 2002) yet they did not meet criteria for ASD, nor did they show evidence of either language delays or delays in general development. Ben-Yizhak and colleagues (2011) used items from the ADOS and combined them to create "semantic-pragmatic profile scores" (p. 753) which enabled them to compare language performance among the three subsets of youngsters in their study. They learned that ASD siblings with the BAP had less pragmatic language ability than the other two groups of children, even though the BAP children did have adequate academic achievement and reading ability.

However, a study by Levy and Bar-Yuda (2011) reached a different conclusion and argued that "language deficits may not be part of the Broad Autism Phenotype" (p. 341). These investigators tested siblings of nonverbal children with ASD and siblings of typically developing children, using age-appropriate versions of an instrument called the Clinical Evaluation of Language Fundamentals (CELF; Semel, Wiig, & Secord, 1995; Wiig, Secord, & Semel, 1992). Although the two groups of participants obtained significantly different scores on the CELF, these differences became nonsignificant once the participants' full-scale and performance IQ scores were taken into account. In addition, there were no significant differences found in spontaneous speech samples that were obtained from both groups. Levy and Bar-Yuda (2011) highlighted the fact that the participants in their study had siblings with ASD who were nonverbal. Therefore, they disputed the notion that language impairments are a heritable component of ASD.

The results of Levy and Bar-Yuda (2011) stand in contrast to the findings of most other studies that have explored language capabilities in relation to the BAP. The majority of such inquiries seem to support the idea that the BAP includes language deficits among its features. Still, it may be wise to heed the note of caution voiced by Cruz et al. (2013), who expressed a need for further studies to confirm the notion that language impairment is a definite characteristic of the BAP

5.5. INTELLECTUAL FUNCTIONING

As stated by Le Couteur et al. (1996), "It has long been appreciated that autism is associated with a very wide range of IQ ..." (p. 795). These researchers were among the first to investigate IQ performance in connection with the BAP. They assessed intellectual functioning among twin pairs in which one twin had the BAP but the other twin did not. As their measure of verbal IQ, Le Couteur and colleagues employed the British Picture Vocabulary Scale (BPVS; Dunn, Dunn, Whetton, & Pintillie, 1982). They used a Wechsler intelligence test (Wechsler, 1974, 1981) to gauge nonverbal IQ.

Le Couteur et al. (1996) discovered that twins with the BAP had a mean nonverbal IQ score within the average range, whereas the mean verbal IQ score was below average and nearly 20 points lower than the nonverbal IQ score. However, other patterns of performance were noted in a review by Bailey et al. (1998). Some of the studies cited in the 1998 review article reported findings similar to those obtained by Le Couteur et al. (1996), with the verbal IQ of individuals with ASD siblings falling noticeably below their nonverbal IQ. However, other early investigations claimed that intellectual functioning for parents and siblings of individuals with ASD was better than that of control participants. Thus, Bailey et al. (1998) decided that "There is no consistent evidence across studies for either general cognitive impairment or advantage among relatives" (p. 377).

An early empirical study of intellectual functioning in the BAP (Folstein et al., 1999) recruited parents and siblings of people with ASD and compared their intellectual ability to that of parents and siblings of individuals with Down syndrome. No significant differences were found between the two groups of siblings, but a comparison of the two groups of parents did yield significant differences. Both of the parent groups demonstrated above average intelligence as measured by the Wechsler Adult Intelligence Scale-Revised (WAIS-R; Wechsler, 1981) Full Scale IQ. However, in comparison to parents of youngsters with Down syndrome, the parents of children with ASD obtained significantly lower scores on the Full Scale IQ and Performance IQ. Another noteworthy finding in this study was the relationship between early language delays and IQ. Parents of children with ASD who themselves had a history of childhood language delays produced significantly lower verbal IQ scores. In contrast, parents of children with ASD and without a personal history of language delay were frequently observed to have verbal IQ scores that were more than one standard deviation higher than their Performance IQ scores. Based on these results, Folstein et al. (1999) speculated that intellectual functioning in the BAP relates to language ability and is distinct from social aspects of the BAP.

Several recent studies have focused on intellectual functioning in siblings of ASD children. For example, Pilowsky, Yirmiya, Gross-Tsur, and Shalev (2007) compared siblings of children with ASD to siblings of children with either intellectual impairment or developmental language delay. The youngsters who participated in this investigation completed the Wechsler Intelligence Scale for Children-Third edition (WISC-III; Wechsler, 1991). Only one significant difference emerged from the statistical analyses performed during this study. Children whose siblings had ASD had significantly higher verbal IQ scores than the participants whose siblings had developmental language delays (Pilowsky et al., 2007).

Five-year-olds who had older siblings with ASD served as the focus of inquiry in a study by Warren and colleagues (2012). This longitudinal investigation also included children who had neurotypical older siblings, and began when all participants were 2 years of age. Intellectual ability was determined on the basis of participants' scores on the Differential Ability Scales-Second Edition (DAS-II; Elliott, 2007). The two groups of children did not differ significantly in Global Conceptual Ability (GCA) but group differences approached significance; participants whose older siblings had ASD produced lower GCA scores on the DAS than participants with typically developing older siblings (Warren et al., 2012).

Yet another longitudinal study (Georgiades et al., 2012) tracked infants who had older siblings with ASD, deeming these children to be at high risk of eventually meeting criteria for either ASD or the BAP. Low-risk infants with no family history of ASD served as a comparison group. Participants from both groups had full-term gestational periods and no obvious developmental disorders. They entered the study around 12 months of age and were reevaluated when they were 3 years old. This project utilized the Early Learning Composite from the Mullen Scales of Early Learning (MSEL; Mullen, 1995) as its measure of intellectual ability. Georgiades et al. (2012) also incorporated a semi-structured instrument called the Autism Observation Scale for Infants (AOSI; Bryson, Zwaigenbaum, McDermott, Rombough, & Brian, 2008) to examine whether the infants in this study displayed features resembling ASD.

Cluster analyses of AOSI data in the study by Georgiades and associates (2012) yielded two clusters: high risk and low risk for ASD. Infants in the high-risk cluster exhibited more ASD-like traits when they reached 3 years of age. Furthermore, they had lower levels of intellectual functioning according to their scores on the Early Learning Composite of the MSEL. The authors of this study warned, "We cannot yet confirm that these are the same children who present with the BAP at later ages" (Georgiades et al., 2012, p. 46). Nevertheless, they followed by stating that the high-risk children in their study might be demonstrating early indications of the BAP.

As shown by the studies described in this section, intellectual functioning in the BAP appears to vary considerably. Some reports have claimed that the BAP is characterized by below-average intellectual ability while others have suggested that individuals with the BAP function in the average to high average range of intelligence (Gerdts & Bernier, 2011). Persons with the BAP also appear likely to manifest considerable variability in cognitive functioning, such as visual-spatial skills that exceed language and vocabulary skills (Gerdts & Bernier, 2011).

5.6. EXECUTIVE FUNCTIONING

A number of studies have explored the ability of individuals with the BAP in the realm of executive functioning. This term encompasses such mental abilities as working memory, planning, cognitive flexibility, and response inhibition (Goussé et al., 2002). Several authors have cited previous research indicating that relatives of individuals with ASD have deficits in planning and cognitive flexibility (e.g., Bailey et al., 1998; Cruz et al., 2013; Gerdts & Bernier, 2011; Goussé et al., 2002). However, it seems that different investigations have yielded disparate findings.

For example, in a study by Wong, Maybery, Bishop, Maley, and Hallmayer (2006), parents and siblings of people with ASD were administered the Tower of London test (ToL; Culbertson & Zillmer, 1998) to assess planning ability and the IDED set-shifting task (Owen et al., 1993) to measure cognitive flexibility. The ToL test requires participants to build towers using colored disks and wooden posts, so that the assembled towers looks like images provided on stimulus cards. The towers are of increasing complexity and must be built within a specified minimum number of moves of the materials. The IDED task is a computer-administered assessment to check for either perseverative thinking or difficulty in reverting attention to something that previously was irrelevant (Wong et al., 2006). Wong and associates (2006) discovered that neither siblings nor parents of ASD probands evinced noteworthy problems with planning or mental flexibility. Based on their results, these authors determined that "the broad autism phenotype may not be characterized primarily by impairments in planning and cognitive flexibility, as had been previously proposed" (p. 561).

Another study (Pilowsky et al., 2007) included the Tower of Hanoi test (ToH; Borys, Spitz, & Dorans, 1982) to examine planning ability. Similar to the ToL described earlier, the ToH requires the test-taker to move a tower of disks from one wooden peg to another, following a prescribed set of instructions (e.g., a larger disk cannot be placed on top of a smaller disk). Participants first received a three-disk tower; if they successfully accomplished this task, they were then given a four-disk tower to complete. They were scored according to the time and number of moves needed to complete each task. In the study by Pilowsky et al. (2007), participants included siblings of children with ASD, siblings of children with intellectual disability, and siblings of children with developmental language delays. Similar to the findings of Wong et al. (2006), no significant differences emerged among these three groups on the ToH as a measure of planning ability, nor on any of the other neuropsychological tests that were administered during this study (Pilowsky et al., 2007).

Younger siblings of children with ASD and younger siblings of typically developing children participated in a longitudinal study by Warren et al. (2012) that began when the children were 2 years old. When these two groups of youngsters reached 5 years of age, they completed subtests of the NEPSY-II (Korkman, Kirk, & Kemp, 2007) that examined their executive functioning. These subtests included measures of auditory attention, motor persistence, and response inhibition, the scores for which were combined to create an Executive Functioning Composite score. As reported in this study, siblings of children with ASD obtained significantly lower Executive Functioning Composite scores. Follow-up analyses further revealed that this difference was mainly due to lower scores on an auditory attention subtest for youngsters whose older siblings had ASD (Warren et al., 2012).

Because executive functions include working memory ability, Gokcen, Bora, Erermis, Kesikci, and Aydin (2009) examined verbal working memory in parents of children with ASD by using a test call the Auditory Consonant Trigrams (ACT; Lezak, 2004). This procedure involves reading three consonants to the test-taker, who then must count backwards from a specified number and later repeat the consonants. Results yielded significant differences, with parents of children with ASD obtaining lower scores on the ACT in comparison to parents of neurotypical children. Gokcen et al. (2009) hypothesized that working memory deficits among unaffected relatives of probands with ASD suggest "the possibility of a genetically mediated deficit" (p. 51).

Parents of individuals with ASD, as well as adults with ASD and volunteers from a nonclinical adult population, partook in a study by Grove, Baillie, Allison, Baron-Cohen, and Hoekstra (2013) that compared participants' ability for systemizing, which the authors defined as "the drive to understand and derive rules about a system" (p. 601). Because systemizing involves concept formation, it is a type of executive functioning (Fine et al., 2009). Participants in the Grove et al. (2013) study completed the Systemizing Quotient-Revised (SQ-R; Wheelwright et al., 2006), a 75-item self-report instrument that asks respondents to indicate their level of agreement with each item. An example of an item in the SQ-R is "When I learn about a new category I like to go into detail to understand the small differences between different members of that category" (Grove et al., 2013, p. 602). Scores on the SQ-R range from 0 to 150, with higher scores indicative of greater systemizing. Previous research had shown that in comparison to a control group, people with ASD tend to produce higher scores on the SQ-R. However, results of the 2013 study by Grove et al. found no significant differences between parents of children with ASD and controls in terms of SQ-R scores. Also, both of these groups obtained lower SQ-R scores relative to the scores of adults with ASD (Grove et al., 2013).

A community-based sample of young and middle-aged adults provided data for an investigation of cognitive flexibility performed by Gokcen, Petrides, Hudry, Frederickson, and Smillie (2014). ASD features in these individuals were measured using the AQ, enabling the researchers to divide the participant sample into high AQ and low AQ groups. Gokcen et al. (2014) evaluated participants' cognitive flexibility by administering the Wisconsin Card Sorting Test (WCST; Grant & Berg, 1948). During the WCST, the test-taker must sort cards according to various attributes of each card, such as its color, design, or the position of a design on the card face. The respondent is provided feedback concerning whether each card has been sorted correctly, and on the basis of the feedback, he or she must learn the way to sort the cards on a trial-and-error basis. Following 10 correct responses, the criteria for card-sorting changes, thus requiring the test-taker to make a mental shift and apply a new rule for sorting the cards.

Gokcen and colleagues (2014) employed a previously published method to calculate shifting efficiency in order to quantify and compare participants' performances on the WCST. They learned that the high AQ participants demonstrated significantly lower performance on this test in comparison to the performance of low AQ group members. These authors concluded that ASD traits are associated with problems in cognitive flexibility (Gokcen et al., 2014).

Much like the findings about the intellectual ability of individuals with the BAP, recent studies concerning executive functioning in the BAP paint an inconsistent picture. Some investigations suggest that the BAP includes deficits in attention, planning, working memory, and cognitive flexibility while others imply the opposite. Clearly, more research is needed to determine whether or not impairments in executive functioning should be considered a basic aspect of the BAP.

5.7. CENTRAL COHERENCE

The theory of central coherence often has been used to explain cognitive features of ASD. The term *central coherence* refers to an ability to see a picture or object as a whole, without getting lost in miniscule details (Gerdts & Bernier, 2011). Some researchers have proposed that individuals with ASD have weak central coherence, meaning that they tend to fixate on parts rather than on an entire object (Gerdts & Bernier, 2011). However, inconsistent findings have been reported in the scientific literature concerning weak central coherence as an attribute of the BAP, depending on whether visual or verbal skills were being assessed (Cruz et al., 2013).

Two early studies of central coherence in the BAP (Briskman, Happé, & Frith, 2001; Happé, Briskman, & Frith, 2001) recruited parents and male siblings of boys with ASD as participants. Boys with dyslexia and neurotypical boys comprised the comparison groups in both studies. In the first of these two investigations, Happé et al. (2001) asked participants to complete four measures of central coherence: the Un/segmented Block Design task (Shah & Frith, 1993), the Embedded Figures Test (EFT; Witkin, Oltman, Raskin, & Karp, 1971), a visual illusions test (Happé, 1996), and a sentence completion task (Booth & Happé, 2010; Happé, 2000). The first two of these experimental tasks entailed visual problem-solving, the third task evaluated perceptual reasoning, and the final task involved semantic language. All of these measures examined whether the respondents exhibited tendencies to perceive individual parts rather than to derive meaning from an entire context. When Happé and colleagues (2001) analyzed their data they found that parents of children with ASD, especially fathers, demonstrated a preference for focusing on details within all four experimental tests. Therefore, they surmised that weak central coherence might be a feature of the BAP.

A follow-up study (Briskman et al., 2001) used parental self-reports and parents' ratings of their children to evaluate the role of central coherence in everyday life circumstances. The authors hypothesized that participants who had displayed weak central coherence in their initial study (i.e., Happé et al., 2001) would be highly skilled at detail-oriented tasks and would manifest piecemeal cognitive processing rather than global, contextual cognitive processing in daily life situations. This inquiry revealed no differences between male siblings of boys with ASD and the boys in either of the two control groups (i.e., boys with dyslexia and neurotypical boys). However, parents of sons with ASD differed from parents of healthy sons and parents whose sons had dyslexia. Parents of sons with ASD, who had obtained high scores regarding nonsocial real-life questions, showed weaker central coherence as measured by the experimental tasks that were administered in the preceding study by Happé et al. (2001). Furthermore, 78% of the fathers of ASD sons worked in detail-oriented professions such as engineering, accounting, and computing; these same participants also were found to have weak central coherence on the basis of their self-report responses as well as the experimental tasks in the first study. Therefore, Briskman et al. (2001) suggested that the BAP includes a component that they referred to as "folk physics" (p. 313), by which they meant that weak central coherence facilitates performance in tasks requiring "spatial, mathematical, and technical abilities" (p. 313).

Losh et al. (2009) also investigated the issue of central coherence within a neuropsychological study of the BAP. These authors reported that the right hemisphere of the brain governs integrative processing, while the left hemisphere is associated with the cognitive processing of individual features rather than a global gestalt. Participants in the Losh et al. (2009) research project included people with high-functioning ASD, a corresponding group of neurotypical controls, parents of individuals with ASD, and a group of neurotypical parents whose children had no history of developmental delays. Measures of central coherence completed by these participants were the EFT as well as the same Sentence Completion task and Block Design task that Happé et al. (2001) had used. Results uncovered no group differences between the ASD parent group and the other parent groups on either the EFT or the Block Design task. For the Sentence Completion task, the only observed difference was that parents of individuals with ASD, regardless of BAP status, provided significantly more rapid responses to the test items than controls did. Consequently, Losh and associates (2009) decided that central coherence was not particularly useful as a distinguishing characteristic of individuals with the BAP.

A 2011 study by Nyden, Hagberg, Goussé, and Rastam looked at central coherence in families with multiple incidences of ASD. Eighteen families, each of which contained at least two members with ASD, underwent neuropsychological assessment. Similar to several other studies already mentioned in this section, Nyden et al. (2011) utilized the EFT as their measure of central coherence. To complete this test, respondents must be able to correctly identify a simple design that is embedded within a larger, more complex design. Although children with ASD who participated in this study did demonstrate weak central coherence, the same could not be said for either their parents or their siblings. Therefore, like Losh et al. (2009) before them, Nyden et al. (2011) also stated that weak central coherence does not appear to be a feature of the BAP.

In accordance with what had been reported by Cruz et al. (2013), it cannot yet be determined with certainty whether weak central coherence is a standard part of the BAP. Some studies find evidence of weak central coherence among parents of persons with ASD, while others report no such evidence. Additionally, no studies reported weak central coherence among people whose siblings had ASD. It appears as though weak central coherence is not a definite feature of the BAP. Alternatively, its presence may depend on either on the type of assessment used to detect it, or on whether the task being completed is verbal or nonverbal.

5.8. THEORY OF MIND (TOM)

Cruz et al. (2013) claimed that Theory of Mind (ToM) is "the main cognitive model of the social impairments of individuals with autism-spectrum disorder" (p. 260). The term *theory of mind* refers to the ability to identify one's own mental state and to infer the mental states of others. This ability consists of perceiving another person's state of mind by observing facial expressions and bodily motions, but also includes reasoning about someone's state of mind by considering the situational context in connection with prior knowledge of that person (Cruz et al., 2013). ToM enables someone to explain and predict other people's beliefs, desires, intentions, and behaviors (Chevallier, Kohls, Troiani, Brodkin, & Schultz, 2012). Deficits in ToM contribute to a lack of pretend play in children, as well as impaired empathy and interpersonal difficulties (Cruz et al., 2013).

ToM has been studied in siblings and parents of people with ASD, and in individuals from a general population who are high in ASD traits. For example, Shaked, Gamliel, and Yirmiya (2006) evaluated young siblings of children with ASD in comparison to an age-matched group of typically developing children. All participants were approximately 4.6 years old. Both groups were similar in terms of intelligence, language ability, and adaptive skills, and had parents who were comparable in terms of age and educational attainment.

Shaked et al. (2006) employed two types of ToM tasks in their investigation. The first of these was a "false belief task" (Shaked et al., 2006, p. 177) in which a male doll and a female doll were shown as if playing with a ball. The female doll placed the ball in a basket and left, after which the male doll moved the ball. In one instance, the ball was placed inside a box belonging to the male doll, and in another instance the ball was hidden inside the pocket of the examiner. When the female doll was returned to the scenario, the participant was asked three questions. The first question dealt with where the female doll would think that the ball was located. The second question asked where the female doll had put the ball before she left, to check that the participant correctly remembered this information. The third question inquired about the current location of the ball. Scores for the false belief task ranged from 0 (failure of both trials) to 2 (correct responses to all three questions for both trials).

The second type of ToM task in the Shaked et al. (2006) study involved the three simplest stories from a battery of nine increasingly difficult "strange stories" created by Happé (1994). These stories described commonplace social interactions in which people said things that were not supposed to be taken literally. After each story, the examiner asked each participant whether something said in the story was true and why a character in the story would say such a thing. The latter was referred to as a justification question. Participants were scored according to the quality of their responses to the justification questions. An incorrect justification received 0 points. A correct justification citing the appearance or behavior of a character in a story earned 1 point, while a justification involving a character's thoughts, feelings, or attitudes received 2 points. Summary scores for the strange stories were combined with participants' scores for the false belief task, thus generating scores for ToM ability.

Data from the Shaked et al. (2006) study revealed no significant differences between siblings of children with ASD and children with neurotypical siblings regarding ToM ability. As a result, the authors wondered whether parents of children with ASD might be deficient in ToM and might transmit this deficit to their children with ASD but not to their unaffected children.

Younger siblings of children with ASD again served as participants in a study by Gliga et al. (2014). Rather than relying on verbal responses, this team of researchers tracked youngsters' eye movements as a means of examining the relationship between the BAP and ToM. Gliga and colleagues (2014) chose to employ this methodology in order to examine the ability to predict another person's actions, apart from language ability. Their participants came from a British longitudinal study of 3-year-old children at risk for ASD due to having an older sibling already diagnosed with ASD. Members of the control group were children recruited from a database of healthy volunteers, all of whom had at least one older sibling.

Visual stimuli for the eye-tracking tasks consisted of video footage showing five events. The first two events were included to familiarize participants with the experimental task. During these first two trials, an actress reached through a small window of a toy house for a toy strawberry that was placed either to the left or the right of two boxes that sat in the center of the image. Two and a half seconds prior to this occurrence, each participant received auditory and visual cues; the windows of the room in the video lit up and a chime rang. The actress in the video wore a visor to hide her eyes from view, thereby preventing the participant from using the actress's eyes as a visual cue directed toward where she intended to reach for the toy. These two trials were included in the procedure to teach participants that the actress's goal was to reach for the toy strawberry, and to show them that an audiovisual cue preceded the opening of one of the windows (Gliga et al., 2014).

These two initial trials were followed by two true belief trials and one false belief trial. At the start of a true belief trial, a monkey puppet put a banana in either the left box or the right box inside the little house. Once the puppet left the scene and 2.5 seconds after the audiovisual cue was given, the actress reached through a window behind the box containing the banana and took it. During the false belief trial, this procedure was modified as follows. The actress turned away from the scene, after which the monkey puppet removed the banana from the box on the right, thereby giving rise to a false belief in the actress. Once the audiovisual cue was given, the scene remained static for 5 more seconds (Gliga et al., 2014).

The same video footage was shown to all participants, each of whom was seated on a chair about 60 cm away from the eye-tracking monitor.

The youngsters were told that they were going to be shown a film about a mischievous monkey. One of the researchers stood behind each child during this process and redirected the child to look at the video if he or she became distracted (Gliga et al., 2014).

Gliga et al. (2014) created a calculation to determine the amount of time that each participant looked at the correct or incorrect window in the video. For the false belief trial, a correct response involved a participant's gaze being directed toward the window nearest where the actress believed the banana to be. Although control children in this study performed at better than chance levels, the children in the at-risk group performed at only the level of chance. This finding held true regardless of whether or not the at-risk group members later received a diagnosis of ASD. Differences in gaze behavior from one group to the other were unrelated to general intelligence and verbal ability. Furthermore, eye-tracking data confirmed that group differences in gaze direction could not be accounted for by failure to attend to visually relevant information. Therefore, Gliga and colleagues (2014) wrote that "difficulties with using mental state understanding for action prediction may be an endophenotype of autism spectrum disorders" (p. 903).

These results contrast with the findings of Nyden et al. (2011) who studied ToM in 18 multiple-incidence ASD families, each containing two or more family members diagnosed with ASD. These scientists used a cartoon explanation task to measure ToM in children and adults. Some of the cartoons based their humor on factors unrelated to ToM (such as being physically absurd), while the humor in other cartoons depended on understanding the mental state (e.g., false beliefs) of characters shown in them. Nyden and associates defined ToM impairment as good ability to explain nonmental cartoons but deficient performance in explaining cartoons based on mental humor. They devised standard scores for the cartoon explanation task, but analyses of these scores revealed no specific problems in participants' understanding of cartoons that relied on ToM ability to comprehend their humorous content. According to Nyden et al. (2011), the cartoon task may have not have been sensitive enough to detect subtle problems in ToM. Nevertheless, they concluded that ToM deficits could not be confirmed as an element of the BAP.

Some recent studies have focused on the ToM ability of parents whose children have ASD. In one such study, Losh and Piven (2007) gave the Reading the Mind from the Eyes Test (more commonly known as simply the Eyes Test; Baron-Cohen, Wheelwright, Hill et al., 2001) to 48 parents of children with ASD and 22 control parents. Sixteen of the parents in the control group had typically developing children; the other six parents in the control group had children with Down syndrome. Parents were evaluated to determine their BAP status through administration of the M-PAS-R (Piven et al., 1997), the Friendship Interview (Piven et al., 1997), and the PRS (Piven et al., 1997). On the basis of these measures, parents of children with ASD were classified as aloof, rigid, or non-BAP (i.e., BAP —).

The Eyes Test demands that participants identify the correct emotion from a list of four possible choices for each photograph, which shows only the eyes area of a face. When Losh and Piven (2007) reviewed their results, they noticed that most parents of children with ASD were unimpaired on the Eyes Test. However, those parents of children with ASD who had been classified as aloof were significantly impaired in correctly identifying the emotional states depicted in the Eyes Test stimuli. (Interestingly, parents of ASD children who had been identified as rigid, rather than aloof, did not manifest these difficulties.) Losh and Piven (2007) also discovered that poor performance on the Eyes Test correlated with pragmatic language difficulties and low-quality friendships. They interpreted the outcome of their study as evidence that impaired ToM on the Eyes Test is a concomitant of the BAP and a potential endophenotype for ASD (Losh & Piven, 2007).

In another such investigation, Gokcen et al. (2009) recruited 76 parents of youngsters with ASD and compared them to 41 parents of typically developing children, using four different approaches to examine ToM. Two of these methods, the Faces Test and the Eyes Test, allowed the researchers to gain information about participants' ability to decode someone's mental state. Two other tests, the Unexpected Outcomes Test (UOT) and the Hinting task, provided information about the respondents' capacity to engage in reasoning about another person's mental state.

Gokcen and colleagues (2009) administered the first 10 photographs of the Faces Test (Adolphs, Baron-Cohen, & Tranel, 2002), which asks each participant to identify the emotions shown in the photographs. These depicted the seven basic emotions of happiness, sadness, fear, surprise, anger, disgust, and distress. For each photograph, participants were provided with two possible choices and were asked to choose one of these two emotions, earning one point for each correct response. Similarly, participants completed the first 27 stimuli from the previously described Eyes Test (Baron-Cohen, Wheelwright, Hill et al., 2001).

When taking the UOT (Dyck, Ferguson, & Shochet, 2001), each participant read 12 brief stories about situations that would have evoked an emotion in one of the stories' characters; however, the emotional reaction described in each story did not match the story's context. Therefore, each participant had to think about the emotions in each story and provide more information to explain and resolve the incongruous emotions. This test was used to assess the participants' ability for empathy (Gokcen et al., 2009).

Four stories comprised the Hinting task (Corcoran, Mercer & Frith, 1995; Janssen, Krabbendam, Jolles, & Van Os, 2003). In these stories, one character interacts with another. At the conclusion of each story, the character hints about an intention and the participant must infer what the character meant.

A review of results obtained by Gokcen et al. (2009) indicated that the parents of children with ASD performed as well as the control parents on three of the four ToM tests. The exception was the UOT, on which they performed significantly worse than the control group. For this reason, the authors believed that "ToM deficits and empathy dysfunction should be investigated as potential endophenotypes in autism" (p. 51).

The Eyes Test (described earlier in this chapter), as well as a Morphed Faces Task, measured ToM in Losh et al.'s (2009) neuropsychological study of the BAP. During the Morphed Faces Task, participants were shown neutral faces that were gradually modified (i.e., morphed) into increasing approximations of sadness, happiness, or fear. Faces that have undergone little morphing are very similar to neutral faces and convey only a minimal amount of emotion. Performance on this test was scored according to previously published norms (Adolphs & Tranel, 2004).

In Losh et al.'s (2009) study, 22 parents of children with ASD were rated as socially aloof; this group was referred to as BAP+. Another 34 parents of children with ASD were considered to have BAP features of perfectionism and rigidity, and 40 parents of children with ASD were classified as not having the BAP (i.e., BAP−). Additionally, 32 parents of typically developing children served as controls in this investigation. The BAP+ group performed significantly less well on the Eyes Test when compared to BAP− and control parents. On the Morphed Faces Task, BAP+ parents performed significantly less well than the rigid BAP parents, BAP− parents, and control parents with regard to identifying fearfulness at low levels of morphing. However, no significant differences were found regarding happy or sad faces. The authors consequently reported that neither central coherence nor executive functions seemed to differentiate the BAP whereas the ToM tasks distinguished the BAP+ parents from the other parent groups in their study (Losh et al., 2009).

More recently, the Eyes Test and an auditory variation of that test allowed Tajmirriyahi, Nenati, Pouretemad, and Sepehr (2013) to evaluate

ToM ability in parents of children with ASD, parents whose children had Down syndrome, and parents of neurotypical children. In addition to the Eyes Test, this team of researchers used a procedure called Reading the Mind in the Voice, or the Voice Test (Rutherford, Baron-Cohen, & Wheelwright, 2002). According to Tajmirriyahi et al. (2013), previous studies had demonstrated that people with ASD struggle when attempting to obtain information about others' mental states by listening to verbal statements. The investigators were interested in learning whether parents of individuals with ASD would manifest similar problems. Participants in this study listened to statements from the Voice Test via headphones, and were permitted to listen to each vocal segment as many as three times.

Adults who partook in the Tajmirriyahi et al. (2013) inquiry were comparable with regard to age and intelligence. The three groups of participants were similar in their performance on the Eyes Test but did produce significantly different results on the Voice Test. Post-hoc analyses indicated that the parents of youngsters with ASD performed significantly worse on the Voice Test than did parents of children with Down syndrome or parents of typically developing children. Thus, Tajmirriyahi and colleagues (2013) asserted that "deficits in mind-reading from voice could also be a part of BAP" (p. 1543).

ToM ability within the BAP also has been examined using participants from a general population who are high in ASD traits. Eriksson (2013) recruited a sample of 600 community-dwelling online participants from the United States to focus on the mental processing of humor as a way to evaluate ToM. This author noted that individuals with ASD often have an odd sense of humor; their poor ToM ability has been linked with a failure to comprehend the humor in false statements, as well as inability to appreciate humor in cartoons involving intentions and mental states of cartoon characters. Participants in Eriksson's (2013) study ranged in age from 18 to 88 years old; more than half of them were college-educated. They completed the AQ as a measure of ASD traits, and a humor styles questionnaire that assessed four different types of humor: affiliative, aggressive, self-enhancing, and self-defeating. Two of these humor styles, affiliative and self-enhancing, were characterized as positive because they allow for relationship-building or are benign. The other two humor styles, self-defeating and aggressive, were labeled as negative because they use humor at the expense of either self or others (Eriksson, 2013).

Statistical analyses conducted by Eriksson (2013) showed a negative correlation between AQ scores and both of the positive humor styles. Although there were no differences between high- and low-AQ groups for negative humor, participants who obtained high scores on the AQ scored significantly lower than low-AQ participants on measures of affiliative and self-enhancing humor. As further noted by the author of this study, "poor mind-reading skills were linked to aggressive and self-defeating humor styles" (Eriksson, 2013, p. 471). Eriksson (2013) expressed a belief that the findings of this study lent support for the existence of the BAP within the general population.

Once again, contradictory results appear within the literature, this time regarding ToM ability in persons with the BAP. Although several studies do imply that the BAP includes deficits in ToM, other investigations claim that this is not the case. Additional research will need to use larger samples and other kinds of measures to more clearly decide whether ToM impairment is an element of the BAP.

5.9. SOCIAL COGNITION

ToM is one component of a broader skill known as social cognition (Losh et al., 2009). *Social cognition* includes "... the processing of emotional information, perception of social cues, and ability to mentalize and make judgments about social relationships" (Gokcen et al., 2014, p. 187). As Happé and Frith (2014) stated, "ASD is the clinical diagnosis most clearly linked to deficits in automatic mental state attribution and related processes" (p. 569). This fact has led some researchers to explore whether impaired social cognition also might be common among persons who fit the definition of the BAP.

In addition to the Eyes Test and the Morphed Faces Test, both of which have already been discussed in this chapter, Losh et al.'s (2009) neuropsychological study of the BAP incorporated three other instruments for the assessment of social cognition. The Trustworthiness of Faces task (Adolphs, Tranel, & Damasio, 1998) asks participants to gauge the trustworthiness of faces that vary according to sex, gaze direction, emotion, and other factors. The Movie Stills Task (Adolphs & Tranel, 2003) is a norms-based measure that requires respondents to use facial expressions of emotion to understand complicated scenes. In this test, some of the still movie scenes are shown with the actors' faces having been erased digitally; in other scenes, facial expressions of anger, sadness, or fear are included. The third measure was the Point Light Task (Heberlein, Adolphs, Tranel, & Damasio, 2004), involving participants' ability to make judgments about emotions suggested by moving points of light that are emitted from diodes attached to the bodies of moving people. The accuracy of judgments about basic emotions as well as trustworthiness judgments were evaluated and scored according to previously established norms.

The Trustworthiness of Faces task revealed that parents of children with ASD who were BAP+ (i.e., socially aloof parents) were significantly more likely than non-BAP parents of ASD children and control parents to rate friendly faces as less trustworthy and mildly threatening. BAP+ parents also performed significantly less accurately than the BAP− parents and control parents on the Movie Stills Task when actors' faces were shown. In other words, BAP− and control parents were able to use actors' facial expressions of emotion to improve their accuracy in interpreting complex movie scenes, while the BAP+ parents did not benefit from such additional information. Regarding the Point Light Task, no between-group differences were found for the identification of basic emotions. However, when making judgments about trustworthiness during this test, the BAP+ group was less sensitive than other parent groups to differences in emotional valence. Control parents and BAP− parents judged positively valenced movements as trustworthy and negatively valenced movements as less trustworthy. In contrast, the BAP+ parents judged both of these types of stimuli to be neutral. On the basis of their results, Losh et al. (2009) concluded that BAP+ parents resembled individuals with ASD in terms of social cognition, even though their performance was similar to that of BAP− and control parents on measures of executive functioning and central coherence.

Sasson, Nowlin, and Pinkham (2012) asserted that impairments in social cognition distinguished BAP+ parents from non-BAP parents more consistently than other types of neuropsychological abilities. They sought to learn whether the social cognition deficits of the BAP could be identified in a general population. Sasson and colleagues (2012) asked 74 undergraduate students to complete the BAPQ (Hurley et al., 2007), which was devised specifically to assess BAP traits. They decided to combine scores from two BAPQ subscales, namely the social abnormalities subscale and the pragmatic language subscale, for use as a composite measure of the social BAP.

Sasson et al. (2012) stated that basic components of social cognition included abilities for face processing, emotion recognition, and ToM. Thus, their investigation included three measures to assess these aspects of social cognition: the Benton Facial Recognition Task (BFRT; Benton et al., 1994), the Penn Emotion Recognition Task (also known as the ER40; Kohler, Bilker, Hagedoorn, Gur, & Gur, 2000), and the Cartoon Theory of Mind test (CTOM; Brunet, Safarti, & Hardy-Bale', 2003). The BFRT presents a black-and-white photograph of a face and asks respondents to choose a matching face from among six options. The task increases in difficulty as the test progresses, due to changes in lighting and orientation of the possible choices for each test item. Sasson and associates (2012) used the ER40 to examine participants' ability to recognize facial expressions of emotion. The ER40 contains 40 color photographs that show neutral faces as well as faces displaying happiness, sadness, fear, and anger. These faces are balanced with regard to gender, ethnicity, age, and type of emotion, and both low- and high-intensity emotional displays are included among its items. The CTOM is comprised of 42 three-panel comic strips, each of which shows a brief story. For each of these items, a respondent must select one of three possible choices as a fourth panel to finish each vignette. Among the three possibilities is an "Attribution of Intentions" option (Sasson et al., 2012, p. 659) that shows a person doing something to achieve a goal. Therefore, correctly choosing the fourth panel for each item involves making a correct inference about the intention of the character in the story. The other two options depend on an understanding of causation, either with or without a human character (Sasson et al., 2012).

The research team calculated Z-scores for the number of correct responses provided by each participant on the BFRT, ER40, and the "Attribution of Intentions" choice within the CTOM. These scores were then averaged to form a social cognition composite variable (Sasson et al., 2012).

A social skill task also was included in the Sasson et al. (2012) inquiry, using an approach called the conversation probe (CP; Penn, Hope, Spaulding, & Kucera, 1994). This method involves a 3-minute videotaped interaction during which an unfamiliar research associate tries to create a natural conversation with each respondent. Participants were told that the goal of the conversation was to become familiar with the research assistant, as if the two of them were meeting for the first time at a party. Instructions for the research confederate were to be pleasant and interactive but to speak for less than half the duration of the assessment, in order to obtain sufficient behavioral data from each participant. Other research assistants later coded the videotaped conversations; they had been trained to achieve a high degree of inter-rater agreement and did not know the BAP status of each participant. The raters evaluated each participant on overall social skill, which included the use of eye contact and appropriate affect as well as degree of engagement in the conversation.

Upon analyzing their data, Sasson and colleagues (2012) found that the composite social BAP scale was inversely correlated with both social skill and the social cognition composite score. Furthermore, participants who were classified as "social BAP positive" displayed less social skill and poorer performance on the tests of social cognition when compared to the "social BAP negative" group. Regression analyses indicated that reduced social skill was partially mediated by impaired ability for social cognition. As a result, Sasson and associates (2012) stated that "aspects of the BAP within the general population are related to reduced real-world social skill" (p. 663). According to these authors, their findings extended the prior research of both Losh and Piven (2007) and Losh et al. (2009) by revealing that social elements of the BAP can be found in the general populace and are linked with reduced ability in social cognition.

The findings of the studies described in this section appear to be in agreement. They indicate that deficits in social cognition are common among people who fit the category of the BAP, and that these deficits are similar to the impaired social cognition of persons with ASD.

5.10. SUMMARY

Many aspects of cognition have been reviewed in this chapter, with the hope of determining which of these abilities is reliably associated with the BAP. Individuals with the BAP may engage in atypical processing of sensory information and they exhibit unusual patterns of visual orienting. Both parents and siblings of individuals with ASD demonstrate problems with recognizing faces, as well as deficits in pragmatic language. Impaired phonological processing may be an element of the BAP, although this is less certain. The level of intellectual functioning is quite varied among people with the BAP, and at this time it is unclear whether deficits in executive functioning, central coherence, or ToM should be considered characteristics of the BAP. However, studies conducted within the past decade appear to indicate that the BAP includes reduced ability for social cognition.

REFERENCES

Adolphs, R., Baron-Cohen, S., & Tranel, D. (2002). Impaired recognition of social emotions following amygdala damage. *Journal of Cognitive Neuroscience*, *14*(8), 1264–1274. doi:10.1162/089892902760807258

Adolphs, R., Spezio, M. L., Parlier, M., & Piven, J. (2008). Distinct face-processing strategies in parents of parents of autistic children. *Current Biology*, *18*(14), 1090–1093. doi:10.1016/j.cub.2008.06.073

Adolphs, R., & Tranel, D. (2003). Amygdala damage impairs emotion recognition from scenes only when they contain facial expressions. *Neuropsychologia, 41*(10), 1281–1289. doi:10.1016/S0028-3932(03)00064-2

Adolphs, R., & Tranel, D. (2004). Impaired judgments of sadness but not happiness following bilateral amygdala damage. *Journal of Cognitive Neuroscience, 16*(3), 453–462. doi:10.1162/089892904322926782

Adolphs, R., Tranel, D., & Damasio, A. R. (1998). The human amygdala in social judgment. *Nature, 393*(6684), 470–474. doi:10.1038/30982

Ahmed, A. A., & Vander Wyk, B. C. (2013). Neural processing of intentional biological motion in unaffected siblings of children with autism spectrum disorder – An fMRI study. *Brain and Cognition, 83*(3), 297–306. doi:10.1016/j.bandc.2013.09.007

Bailey, A., Palferman, S., Heavey, L., & Le Couteur, A. (1998). Autism: The phenotype in relatives. *Journal of Autism and Developmental Disorders, 28*(5), 369–392. doi:10.1023/A:1026048320785

Baron-Cohen, S., Wheelwright, S., Hill, J., Raste, Y., & Plumb, I. (2001). The "Reading the Mind in the Eyes" Test revised version: A study of normal adults, and adults with Asperger syndrome or high-functioning autism. *Journal of Child Psychology and Psychiatry, 42*(2), 241–251. doi:10.1111/1469-7610.00715

Baron-Cohen, S., Wheelwright, S., Skinner, R., Martin, J., & Clubley, E. (2001). The Autism Spectrum Quotient (AQ): Evidence from Asperger syndrome/high-functioning autism, males and females, scientists and mathematicians. *Journal of Autism and Developmental Disorders, 31*(1), 5–17. doi:10.1023/A:1005653411471

Bayliss, A. P., & Kritikos, A. (2011). Brief report: Perceptual load and the autism spectrum in typically developed individuals. *Journal of Autism and Developmental Disorders, 41*(11), 1573–1578. doi:10.1007/s10803-010-1159-8

Belmonte, M. K., Gomot, M., & Baron-Cohen, S. (2010). Visual attention in autism families: 'Unaffected' sibs share atypical frontal activation. *Journal of Child Psychology and Psychiatry, 51*(3), 259–276. doi:10.1111/j.1469-7610.2009.02153.x

Benton, A. L., Sivan, A. B., Hamsher, K. D., Varney, N. R., & Spreen, O. (1994). *Contributions to neuropsychological assessment: A clinical manual* (2nd ed.). New York, NY: Oxford University Press.

Ben-Yizhak, N., Yirmiya, N., Seidman, I., Alom, R., Lord, C., & Sigman, M. (2011). Pragmatic language and school related linguistic abilities in siblings of children with autism. *Journal of Autism and Developmental Disorders, 41*(6), 750–760. doi:10.1007/s10803-010-1096-6

Berument, S. K., Rutter, M., Lord, C., Pickles, A., & Bailey, A. (1999). Autism screening questionnaire: Diagnostic validity. *British Journal of Psychiatry, 175*(5), 444–451. doi:10.1192/bjp.175.5.444

Bishop, D. V. M. (2003). *The children's communication checklist-2*. London: The Psychological Corporation.

Bishop, D. V. M., Maybery, M., Wong, D., Hill, W., & Hallmayer, J. (2004). Are phonological processing deficits part of the broad autism phenotype? *American Journal of Medical Genetics Part B: Neuropsychiatric Genetics, 128B*(1), 54–60. doi:10.1002/ajmg.b.30039

Booth, R., & Happé, F. (2010). "Hunting with a knife and ... fork": Examining central coherence in autism, attention deficit/hyperactivity disorder, and typical development with a linguistic task. *Journal of Experimental Child Psychology, 107*(4), 377–393. doi:10.1016/j.jecp.2010.06.003

Borys, S. V., Spitz, H. H., & Dorans, B. A. (1982). Tower of Hanoi performance of retarded young adults and nonretarded children as a function of solution length and goal state. *Journal of Experimental Child Psychology, 33*(1), 87–110. doi:10.1016/0022-0965(82)90008-X

Briskman, J., Happé, F., & Frith, U. (2001). Exploring the cognitive phenotype of autism: Weak "central coherence" in parents and siblings of children with autism: II. Real-life skills and preferences. *Journal of Psychology and Psychiatry, 42*(3), 309–316. doi:10.1111/1469-7610.00724

Brown, C. E., & Dunn, W. (2002). *Adolescent/adult sensory profile.* San Antonio, TX: Harcourt Assessment, Inc.

Brunet, E., Safarti, Y., & Hardy-Bale', M. C. (2003). Reasoning about physical causality and others' intentions in schizophrenia. *Cognitive Neuropsychiatry, 8*(2), 129–139. doi:10.1080/13546800244000256

Bryson, S. E., Zwaigenbaum, L., McDermott, C., Rombough, V., & Brian, J. (2008). The Autism Observation Scale for Infants: Scale development and reliability data. *Journal of Autism and Developmental Disorders, 38*(4), 731–738. doi:10.1007/s10803-007-0440-y

Chevallier, C., Kohls, G., Troiani, V., Brodkin, E. S., & Schultz, R. T. (2012). The social motivation theory of autism. *Trends in Cognitive Sciences, 16*(4), 231–239. doi:10.1016/j.tics.2012.02.007

Constantino, J. N., & Gruber, C. P. (2005). *Social responsiveness scale.* Los Angeles, CA: Western Psychological Services.

Corcoran, R., Mercer, G., & Frith, C. D. (1995). Schizophrenia, symptomatology and social inference: Investigating theory of mind in people with schizophrenia. *Schizophrenia Research, 17*(1), 5–13. doi:10.1016/0920-9964(95)00024-G

Cruz, L. P., Carmagos-Junior, W., & Rocha, F. L. (2013). The broad autism phenotype in parents of individuals with autism: A systematic review of the literature. *Trends in Psychiatry and Psychotherapy, 35*(4), 252–263. doi:10.1590/2237-6089-2013-0019

Culbertson, W. C., & Zillmer, E. A. (1998). The Tower of London (DX): A standardized approach to assessing executive functioning in children. *Archives of Clinical Neuropsychology, 13*(3), 285–301. doi:10.1016/S0887-6177(97)00033-4

de Klerk, C. C. J. M., Gliga, T., Charman, T., Johnson, M. H., & The BASIS Team. (2014). Face engagement during infancy predicts later face recognition ability in younger siblings of children with autism. *Developmental Science, 17*(4), 596–611. doi:10.1111/desc.12141

De la Marche, W., Steyaert, J., & Noens, I. (2012). Atypical sensory processing in adolescents with an autism spectrum disorder and their non-affected siblings. *Research in Autism Spectrum Disorders, 6*(2), 639–645. doi:10.1016/j.rasd.2011.09.014

Denckla, M. B., & Rudel, R. (1974). Rapid "automatized" naming of pictured objects, colors, letters and numbers by normal children. *Cortex, 10*(2), 186–202. doi:10.1016/S0010-9452(74)80009-2

Duchaine, B., & Nakayama, K. (2006). The Cambridge Face Memory Test: Results for neurologically intact individuals and an investigation of its validity using inverted face stimuli and prosopagnosic participants. *Neuropsychologia, 44*(4), 576–585. doi:10.1016/j.neuropsychologia.2005.07.001

Dunn, L. M., Dunn, L. M., Whetton, C., & Pintillie, D. (1982). *British picture vocabulary scale (manual for long and short forms).* Windsor, UK: NFER Publishers.

Dyck, M. J., Ferguson, K., & Shochet, I. M. (2001). Do autism spectrum disorders differ from each other and from non-spectrum disorders on emotion recognition tests? *European Child and Adolescent Psychiatry, 10*(2), 105–116. doi:10.1007/s007870170033

Dykens, E. M., & Lense, M. (2011). Intellectual disabilities and autism spectrum disorder: A cautionary note. In D. G. Amaral, G. Dawson, & D. H. Geschwind (Eds.), *Autism spectrum disorders* (pp. 263–269). New York, NY: Oxford University Press.

Ekman, P., & Friesen, W. V. (1976). *Pictures of facial affect* [slides]. Palo Alto, CA: Consulting Psychologists Press.

Elison, J. T., Paterson, S. J., Wolff, J. J., Reznick, J. S., Sasson, N. J., Gu, H., ... The IBIS Network. (2013). White matter microstructure and atypical visual orienting in 7-month-olds at risk for autism. *American Journal of Psychiatry, 170*(8), 899–908. doi:10.1176/appi.ajp.2012.12091150

Elliott, C. D. (2007). *Differential ability scales* (2nd ed.). San Antonio, TX: Harcourt Assessment.

Elsabbagh, M., Volein, A., Holmboe, K., Tucker, L., Csibra, G., Baron-Cohen, S., ... Johnson, M. H. (2009). Visual orienting in the early broader autism phenotype: Disengagement and facilitation. *Journal of Child Psychology and Psychiatry, 50*(5), 637–642. doi:10.1111/j.1469-7610.2008.02051.x

Eriksson, K. (2013). Autism-spectrum traits predict humor styles in the general population. *Humor, 26*(3), 461–475. doi:10.1515/humor-2013-0030

Fine, E. M., Delis, D. C., Dean, D., Beckman, V., Miller, B. L., Rosen, H. J., & Kramer, J. H. (2009). Left frontal lobe contributions to concept formation: A quantitative MRI study of D-KEFS sorting test performance. *Journal of Clinical and Experimental Neuropsychology, 31*(5), 624–631. doi:10.1080/13803390802419017

Folstein, S. E., Santangelo, S. L., Gilman, S. E., Piven, J., Landa, R., Lainhart, J., ... Wrozek, M. (1999). Predictors of cognitive test patterns in autism families. *Journal of Child Psychology and Psychiatry, 40*(7), 1117–1128. doi:10.1111/1469-7610.00528

Gallese, V. (2006). Intentional attunement: A neurophysiological perspective on social cognition and its disruption in autism. *Brain Research, 1079*(1), 15–24. doi:10.1016/j.brainres.2006.01.054

Gamliel, I., Yirmiya, N., Jaffe, D. H., Manor, O., & Sigman, M. (2009). Developmental trajectories in siblings of children with autism: Cognition and language from 4 months to 7 years. *Journal of Autism and Developmental Disorders, 39*(8), 1131–1144. doi:10.1007/s10803-009-0727-2

Georgiades, S., Szatmari, P., Zwaigenbaum, L., Bryson, S., Brian, J., Roberts, W., ... Garon, N. (2012). A prospective study of autistic-like traits in unaffected siblings of probands with autism spectrum disorder. *JAMA Psychiatry, 70*(1), 42–48. doi:10.1001/2013.jamapsychiatry.1

Gerdts, J., & Bernier, R. (2011). The broader autism phenotype and its implications on the etiology and treatment of autism spectrum disorders. *Autism Research and Treatment, 2011*, 1–19. (Open access article). Article ID 545901. doi:10.1155/2011/545901

Gliga, T., Senju, A., Pettinato, M., Charman, T., Johnson, M. H., & The BASIS Team. (2014). Spontaneous belief attribution in younger siblings of children on the autism spectrum. *Developmental Psychology, 50*(3), 903–913. doi:10.1037/a0034146

Gokcen, E., Petrides, K. V., Hudry, K., Frederickson, N., & Smillie, L. D. (2014). Subthreshold autism traits: The role of trait emotional intelligence and cognitive flexibility. *British Journal of Psychology, 105*(2), 187–199. doi:10.1111/bjop.12033

Gokcen, S., Bora, E., Erermis, S., Kesikci, H., & Aydin, C. (2009). Theory of mind and verbal working memory in parents of autistic children. *Psychiatry Research, 166*(1), 46–53. doi:10.1016/j.psychres.2007.11.016

Goussé, V., Plumet, M.-H., Chabane, N., Mouren-Simeoni, M.-C., Ferradian, N., & Leboyer, M. (2002). Fringe phenotypes in autism: A review of clinical, biochemical, and cognitive studies. *European Psychiatry, 17*(3), 120–128.

Grandin, T. (2011). Top priorities for autism/Asperger's research: Perspectives from a person with autism. In D. G. Amaral, G. Dawson, & D. H. Geschwind (Eds.), *Autism spectrum disorders* (pp. 1377–1385). New York, NY: Oxford University Press.

Grant, D. A., & Berg, E. (1948). A behavioral analysis of degree of reinforcement and ease of shifting to new responses in Weigl-type card-sorting problem. *Journal of Experimental Psychology, 38*, 404–411.

Grove, R., Baillie, A., Allison, C., Baron-Cohen, S., & Hoekstra, R. A. (2013). Empathizing, systemizing, and autistic traits: Latent structure in individuals with autism, their parents, and general population controls. *Journal of Abnormal Psychology, 122*(2), 600–609. doi:10.1037/a0031919

Happé, F. (2000). *Weak central coherence in autism: Global and local sentence completions.* Manuscript in preparation.

Happé, F. (2005). The weak central coherence account of autism. In F. R. Volkmar, R. Paul, A. Klin, & D. Cohen (Eds.), *Handbook of autism and pervasive developmental disorders* (3rd ed., Vol. 1, pp. 640–649). Hoboken, NJ: Wiley. doi:10.1002./9780470939345.ch24

Happé, F., Booth, R., Charlton, R., & Hughes, C. (2006). Executive function deficits in autism spectrum disorders and attention-deficit/hyperactivity disorder: Examining profiles across domains and ages. *Brain and Cognition, 61*(1), 25–39. doi:10.1016/j.bandc.2006.03.004

Happé, F., Briskman, J., & Frith, U. (2001). Exploring the cognitive phenotype of autism: Weak "central coherence" in parents and siblings of children with autism: I. Experimental tests. *Journal of Child Psychology and Psychiatry, 42*(3), 299–307. doi:10.1111/1469-7610.00723

Happé, F., & Frith, U. (2014). Annual research review: Towards a developmental neuroscience of atypical social cognition. *Journal of Child Psychology and Psychiatry, 55*(6), 553–577. (Open access article). doi:10.1111/jccp.12162

Happé, F. G. E. (1994). An advanced test of theory of mind: Understanding of story characters' thoughts and feelings by able autistic, mentally handicapped, and normal children and adults. *Journal of Autism and Developmental Disorders, 24*(2), 129–153. doi:10.1007/BF02172093

Happé, F. G. E. (1996). Studying weak central coherence at low levels: Children with autism do not succumb to visual illusions. A research note. *Journal of Child Psychology and Psychiatry, 37*(7), 873–877. doi:10.1111/j.1469-7610.1996.tb01483.x

Heberlein, A. S., Adolphs, R., Tranel, D., & Damasio, H. (2004). Cortical regions for judgments of emotions and personality traits from point-light walkers. *Journal of Cognitive Neuroscience, 16*(7), 1143–1158. doi:10.1162/0898929041920423

Hurley, R. S. E., Losh, M., Parlier, M., Reznick, J. S., & Piven, J. (2007). The broad autism phenotype questionnaire. *Journal of Autism and Developmental Disorders, 37*(9), 1679–1690. doi:10.1007/s10803-006-0299-3

Janssen, I., Krabbendam, L., Jolles, J., & Van Os, J. (2003). Alterations in theory of mind in patients with schizophrenia and nonpsychotic relatives. *Acta Psychiatrica Scandinavica, 108*(2), 110–117. doi:10.1034/j.1600-0447.2003.00092.x

Jeffery, L., Rhodes, G., McKone, E., Pellicano, E., Crookes, K., & Taylor, E. (2011). Distinguishing norm-based from exemplar-based coding of identity in children: Evidence from face identity aftereffects. *Journal of Experimental Psychology: Human Perception and Performance, 37*(6), 1824–1840. doi:10.1037/a0025643

Kadak, M. T., Demirel, O. F., Yavuz, M., & Demir, T. (2014). Recognition of emotional facial expressions and broad autism phenotype in parents of children diagnosed with autistic spectrum disorder. *Comprehensive Psychiatry, 55*(5), 1146–1151. doi:10.1016/j.comppsych.2014.03.004

Kohler, C. G., Bilker, W., Hagedoorn, M., Gur, R. E., & Gur, R. C. (2000). Emotion recognition deficit in schizophrenia: Association with symptomatology and cognition. *Biological Psychiatry, 48*(2), 127–136. doi:10.1016/S0006-3223(00)00847-7

Korkman, M., Kirk, U., & Kemp, S. (2007). *The NEPSY-II*. San Antonio, TX: Harcourt Publishing.

Lai, M.-C., Lombardo, M. V., Chakrabarti, B., & Baron-Cohen, S. (2013). Subgrouping the autism "spectrum": Reflections on DSM-5. *PLoS Biology, 11*(4), e1001544. (Open access article). doi:10.1371/journal.pbio.1001544

Landa, R., Piven, J., Wrozek, M. M., Gayle, J. O., Chase, G. A., & Folstein, S. E. (1992). Social language use in parents of autistic individuals. *Psychological Medicine, 22*(1), 245–254. doi:10.1017/S0033291700032918

Le Couteur, A., Bailey, A., Goode, S., Pickles, A., Robertson, S., Gottesman, I., & Rutter, M. (1996). A broader phenotype of autism: The clinical spectrum in twins. *Journal of Child Psychology and Psychiatry, 37*(7), 785–801.

Levy, Y., & Bar-Yuda, C. (2011). Language performance in siblings of nonverbal children with autism. *Autism, 15*(3), 341–354. doi:10.1177/1362361310386504

Lezak, M. D. (2004). *Neuropsychological assessment* (4th ed.). New York, NY: Oxford University Press.

Lord, C., Risi, S., Lambrecht, L., Cook, E. H., Jr., Leventhal, B. L., DiLavore, P. C., ... Rutter, M. (2000). The autism diagnostic observation schedule-generic: A standard measure of social and communication deficits associated with the spectrum of autism. *Journal of Autism and Developmental Disorders, 30*(3), 205–223. doi:10.1023/A:1005592401947

Lord, C., Rutter, M., DiLavore, P. C., & Risi, S. (2002). *Autism diagnostic observation schedule*. Los Angeles, CA: Western Psychological Services.

Losh, M., Adophs, R., Poe, M. D., Couture, S., Penn, D., Baranek, G., & Piven, J. (2009). Neuropsychological profile of autism and the broad autism phenotype. *Archives of General Psychiatry, 66*(5), 518–526. doi:10.1001/archgenpsychiatry.2009.34

Losh, M., Childress, D., Lam, K., & Piven, J. (2008). Defining key features of the broad autism phenotype: A comparison across parents of multiple- and single-incidence autism families. *American Journal of Medical Genetics Part B: Neuropsychiatric Genetics, 147B*, 424–433. doi:10.1002/ajmg.b.30612

Losh, M., Esserman, D., & Piven, J. (2010). Rapid automatized naming as an index of genetic liability to autism. *Journal of Neurodevelopmental Disorders, 2*(2), 109–116. doi:10.1007/s11689-010-9045-4

Losh, M., Klusek, J., Martin, G. E., Sideris, J., Parlier, M., & Piven, J. (2012). Defining genetically meaningful language and personality traits in relatives of individuals with fragile X syndrome and relatives of individuals with autism. *American Journal of Medical Genetics, Part B: Neuropsychiatric Genetics, 159B*(6), 660–668. doi:10.1002/ajmg.b.32070

Losh, M., & Piven, J. (2007). Social-cognition and the broad autism phenotype: Identifying genetically meaningful phenotypes. *Journal of Child Psychology and Psychiatry*, *48*(1), 105–112. doi:10.1111/j.1469-7610.2006.01594.x

Mandy, W., Charman, T., Puura, K., & Skuse, D. H. (2014). Investigating the cross-cultural validity of *DSM-5* autism spectrum disorder: Evidence from Finnish and UK samples. *Autism*, *18*(1), 45–54. doi:10.1177/1362361313508026

McFadden, K. L., Hepburn, S., Winterrowd, E., Schmidt, G. L., & Rojas, D. C. (2012). Abnormalities in gamma-band responses to language stimuli in first-degree relatives of children with autism spectrum disorder: An MEG study. *BMC Psychiatry*, *12*, 213–230. doi:10.1186/1471-244X-12-213

Miu, A. C., Pana, S. E., & Avram, J. (2012). Emotional face processing in neurotypicals with autistic traits: Implications for the broad autism phenotype. *Psychiatry Research*, *198*(3), 489–494. doi:10.1016/j.psychres.2012.01.024

Montagne, B., Kessels, R. P. C., De Haan, E. H. F., & Perrett, D. I. (2007). The emotion recognition task: A paradigm to measure the perception of facial emotional expressions at different intensities. *Perceptual and Motor Skills*, *104*(2), 589–598. doi:10.2466/pms.104.2.589-598

Mullen, E. (1995). *Mullen scales of early learning*. Circle Pines, MN: American Guidance Service.

Nyden, A., Hagberg, B., Goussé, V., & Rastam, M. (2011). A cognitive endophenotype of autism in families with multiple incidence. *Research in Autism Spectrum Disorders*, *5*(1), 191–200. doi:10.1016/j.ras.2010.03.010

Owen, A. M., Roberts, A. C., Hodges, J. R., Summers, B. A., Polkey, C. E., & Robbins, T. W. (1993). Contrasting mechanisms of impaired attentional set-shifting in patients with frontal lobe damage or Parkinson's disease. *Brain*, *116*(Pt. 5), 1159–1175.

Palermo, M. T., Pasqualetti, P., Barbati, G., Intelligente, F., & Rossini, P. M. (2006). Recognition of schematic facial displays of emotion in parents of children with autism. *Autism*, *10*(4), 353–364. doi:10.1177/1362361306064431

Penn, D. L., Hope, D. A., Spaulding, W., & Kucera, J. (1994). Social anxiety in schizophrenia. *Schizophrenia Research*, *11*(3), 277–284. doi:10.1016/0920-9964(94)90022-1

Pilowsky, T., Yirmiya, N., Gross-Tsur, V., & Shalev, R. S. (2007). Neuropsychological functioning of siblings of children with autism, siblings of children with developmental language delay, and siblings of children with mental retardation of unknown genetic etiology. *Journal of Autism and Developmental Disorders*, *37*(3), 537–552. doi:10.1007/s10803-006-0185-z

Piven, J., Palmer, P., Landa, R., Santangelo, S., Jacobi, D., & Childress, D. (1997). Personality and language characteristics in parents from multiple-incidence autism families. *American Journal of Medical Genetics Part B: Neuropsychiatric Genetics*, *74*(4), 398–411. doi:10.1002/(SICI)1096-8628(19970725)74:4 < 398::AID-AJMG11 > 3.0.CO;2-D

Poljac, E., Poljac, E., & Wagemans, J. (2012). Reduced accuracy and sensitivity in the perception of emotional facial expressions in individuals with high autism spectrum traits. *Autism*, *17*(6), 668–680. doi:10.1177/1362361312455703

Raven, J. C., Court, J. H., & Raven, J. (1992). *Standard progressive matrices*. Oxford, UK: Oxford University Press.

Reiersen, A. M., & Todd, R. D. (2008). Co-occurrence of ADHD and autism spectrum disorders: Phenomenology and treatment. *Expert Review of Neurotherapeutics*, *8*(4), 657–669. doi:10.1586/14737175.8.4.657

Rhodes, G., Jeffery, L., Taylor, L., & Ewing, L. (2013). Autistic traits are linked to reduced adaptive coding of face identity and selectively poorer face recognition in men but not women. *Neuropsychologia, 51*(13), 2702–2708. doi:10.1016/j.neuropsychologia.2013.08.016

Rutherford, M. D. (2013). Social attention is measurably and increasingly atypical across the first six months in the broader autism phenotype. *Journal of Psychology & Psychotherapy, 3*(4), 1000125. (Open access article.) doi:10.4172/2161-0487.1000125

Rutherford, M. D., Baron-Cohen, S., & Wheelwright, S. (2002). Reading the mind in the voice: A study with normal adults and adults with Asperger syndrome and high functioning autism. *Journal of Autism and Developmental Disorders, 32*(3), 189–194. doi:10.1023/A:1015497629971

Santangelo, S. L., & Folstein, S. E. (1995). Social deficits in the families of autistic probands. *American Journal of Human Genetics, 57*(4 Suppl.), A20.

Sasson, N. J., Nowlin, R. B., & Pinkham, A. E. (2012). Social cognition, social skill, and the broad autism phenotype. *Autism, 17*(6), 655–667. doi:10.1177/1362361312455704

Scheeren, A. M., & Stauder, J. E. A. (2008). Broader autism phenotype in parents of autistic children: Reality or myth? *Journal of Autism and Developmental Disorders, 38*(2), 276–287. doi:10.1007/s10803-007-0389-x

Schmidt, G. L., Kimel, L. K., Winterrowd, E., Pennington, B. F., Hepburn, S. L., & Rojas, D. C. (2008). Impairments in phonological processing and nonverbal intellectual function in parents of children with autism. *Journal of Clinical and Experimental Neuropsychology, 30*(5), 557–567. doi:10.1080/13803390701551225

Semel, E., Wiig, E. H., & Secord, W. A. (1995). *Clinical evaluation and language fundamentals (CELF)* (3rd ed.). New York, NY: Harcourt, Brace and Company.

Shah, A., & Frith, U. (1993). Why do autistic individuals show superior performance on the Block Design task? *Journal of Child Psychology and Psychiatry, 34*(8), 1351–1364.

Shaked, M., Gamliel, I., & Yirmiya, N. (2006). Theory of mind abilities in young siblings of children with autism. *Autism, 10*(2), 173–187. doi:10.1177/1362361306062023

Tajmirriyahi, M., Nenati, V., Pouretemad, H., & Sepehr, R. M. (2013). Reading the mind in face and voice in parents of children with autism spectrum disorders. *Research in Autism Spectrum Disorders, 7*(12), 1543–1550. doi:10.1016/j.rasd.2013.08.007

Taylor, L. J., Maybery, M. T., Wray, J., Ravine, D., Hunt, A., & Whitehouse, A. J. O. (2013). Brief report: Do the nature of communication impairments in autism spectrum disorders relate to the broader autism phenotype in parents? *Journal of Autism and Developmental Disorders, 43*(12), 2984–2989. doi:10.1007/s10803-013-1838-3

Wahlberg, T. (2001). Cognitive theories and symptomology of autism. In T. Wahlberg, F. Obiakor, S. Burkhardt, & A. F. Rotatori (Eds.), *Autistic spectrum disorders: Educational and clinical interventions* (Vol. 14, pp. 3–17). Oxford, UK: Elsevier Science Ltd. doi:10.1016/S0270-4013(01)80004-0

Wallace, S., Sebastian, C., Pellicano, E., Parr, J., & Bailey, A. (2010). Face processing abilities in relatives of individuals with ASD. *Autism Research, 3*(6), 345–349. doi:10.1002/aur.161

Warren, Z., Foss-Feig, J., Malesa, E., Lee, E., Taylor, J., Newson, C., ... Stone, W. (2012). Neurocognitive and behavioral outcomes of younger siblings of children with autism spectrum disorders at age five. *Journal of Autism and Developmental Disorders, 42*(3), 409–418. doi:10.1007/s10803-011-1263-4

Wechsler, D. (1974). *Manual for the Wechsler intelligence scale for children-revised*. New York, NY: The Psychological Corporation.

Wechsler, D. (1981). *Manual for the Wechsler adult intelligence scale-revised.* New York, NY: The Psychological Corporation.
Wechsler, D. (1991). *Manual for the Wechsler intelligence scale for children (WISC-III)* (3rd ed.). San Antonio, TX: The Psychological Corporation.
Wheelwright, S., Baron-Cohen, S., Goldenfeld, N., Delaney, J., Fine, D., Smith, R., & Wakabayashi, A. (2006). Predicting Autism Spectrum Quotient (AQ) from the Systemizing Quotient-Revised (SQ-R) and Empathy Quotient (EQ). *Brain Research, 1079*(1), 47–56. doi:10.1016/j.brainres.2006.01.012
Whitehouse, A. J. O., Barry, J. G., & Bishop, D. V. M. (2007). The broader language phenotype of autism: A comparison with specific language impairment. *Journal of Child Psychology and Psychiatry, 48*(8), 822–830. doi:10.1111/j.1469-7610.2007.01765.x
Wiig, E. H., Secord, W. A., & Semel, E. (1992). *Clinical evaluation and language fundamentals-preschool (CELF-P).* New York, NY: Harcourt, Brace and Company.
Wilmer, J. B., Germine, L., Chabris, C. F., Chatterjee, G., Williams, M., Loken, E., ... Duchaine, B. (2010). Human face recognition ability is specific and highly heritable. *Proceedings of the National Academy of Sciences, 107*(11), 5238–5241. doi:10.1073/pnas.0913053107
Wilson, C. E., Freeman, P., Brock, J., Burton, A. M., & Palermo, R. (2010). Facial identity recognition in the broader autism phenotype. *PLoS One, 5*(9), e12876. doi:10.1371/journal.pone.0012876
Wilson, L. B., Tregellas, J. R., Slason, E., Pasko, B. E., Hepburn, S., & Rojas, D. C. (2013). Phonological processing in first-degree relatives of individuals with autism: An fMRI study. *Human Brain Mapping, 34*(6), 1447–1463. doi:10.1002/hbm.22001
Witkin, H. A., Oltman, P. K., Raskin, E., & Karp, S. (1971). *A manual for the embedded figure test.* Palo Alto, CA: Consulting Psychologists Press.
Wong, D., Maybery, M., Bishop, D. V. M., Maley, A., & Hallmayer, J. (2006). Profiles of executive function in parents and siblings of individuals with autism spectrum disorders. *Genes, Brain and Behavior, 5*(8), 561–576. doi:10.1111/j.1601-183X.2005.00199.x
Zhu, Q., Song, Y., Hu, S., Li, X., Tian, M., Zhen, Z., ... Liu, J. (2010). Heritability of the specific cognitive ability of face perception. *Current Biology, 20*(2), 137–142. doi:10.1016/j.cub.2009.11.067